The Open University
P933 European Economic Community Block 1 Units 1 and 2
A Post-Experience Course: Prepared by the Course Team

History and Institutions
Unit 1 Laying the Foundations
Unit 2 Community Method

The Open University Press

Introductions, comments and questions on Units 1 and 2
prepared by James Barber and Robert Masterton

This course was devised by a Course Team consisting of:

James Barber, Chairman (Social Science)
Bruce Reed, Deputy Chairman (Post-experience Unit)
Robert Cookson, Editor (Publishing Division)
Chris Cuthbertson, Producer (BBC)
Nicholas Farnes, IET Adviser (Institute of Educational Technology)
Richard Gibbs, Course Assistant (Post-experience Unit)
Robert Masterton, Course Assistant (Post-experience Unit)
Michael Philps, Producer (BBC)
Gail Price, Course Assistant (Post-experience Unit)

The Open University
Walton Hall Milton Keynes

First published 1973. Reprinted 1974
Copyright © 1973 The Open University

Designed by the Media Development Group of The Open University.

Printed in Great Britain by
EYRE AND SPOTTISWOODE LIMITED
AT GROSVENOR PRESS PORTSMOUTH

ISBN 0 335 04720 3

This text forms part of an Open University course. The complete list of units in the course appears at the end of this text.

For general availability of supporting material referred to in this text, please write to the Director of Marketing, The Open University, P.O. Box 81, Milton Keynes MK7 6AT.

Further information on Open University courses may be obtained from the Admissions Office, The Open University, P.O. Box 48, Milton Keynes MK7 6AB.

Unit 1 Laying the Foundations

Unit contents

Section 1
Introduction

Contents

Objectives

Having completed the work for this unit you should be able to:

1 Describe the origins and development of European integration since 1945 and the forces which have operated for and against it.

2 Describe the motives behind this process and identify how some of these motives have changed over time.

3 Examine British attitudes towards European integration since 1945, and how these are related to Britain's changing international position.

4 Summarize the different interpretations of the reasons for Britain joining the EEC presented in the unit.

5 Identify the major European institutions and outline their development.

Set books

Barber, J. and Reed, B. (eds) (1973) *European Community: Vision and Reality*, London, Croom Helm (hereafter referred to as the Reader).

Shonfield, A. (1973) *Europe: Journey to an Unknown Destination*, Harmondsworth, Penguin.

Study programme

Work for week 1	Source of work	Recommended study time
Essential reading in recommended order		
Introduction to Unit 1	Unit 1, Section 1	10 minutes
Britain and the European Communities, 1945–72 *F. S. Northedge*	Unit 1, Section 2	1½ hours
Time-lags in Political Psychology *Uwe Kitzinger*	Unit 1, Section 3; Reader, pp. 7–22	1 hour
The Historical Development of the European Communities *Roy Pryce*	Unit 1, Section 4	2½ hours
Conclusion to Unit 1 and self-assessment activities	Unit 1, Section 5	1 hour
Recommended reading		
'With' them but not 'of' them	Reader, pp. 23–8	
The Great Debate	Reader, pp. 29–42	
Who do we think we are? *Patrick O'Donovan*	Reader, pp. 42–5	

Reference reading

Chronology of events in the formation of the European Communities	Unit 1, Section 6
A glossary of Western European organizations	Unit 1, Section 6
The Communiqué of the Paris Summit, October 1972	Unit 1, Section 6

Broadcasting

Radio Programme 1	BBC VHF radio	20 minutes
Broadcast notes	Supplementary material	20 minutes

Assignment

CMA P933 41 covers Units 1 and 2	Supplementary material	30 minutes

The unit

This unit is intended first, to provide an understanding of the origins and development of European integration between 1945 and 1973, with special reference to Britain's attitude and role, and second, to help in understanding and evaluating future developments by examining the roots from which these developments have grown. This underlines the dynamism of the European integration process, for we are not merely studying the past for its own sake, but in order to understand the processes and developments that are taking place in Europe during the 1970s.

Essential reading

The essential readings for this unit are:

1 'Britain and the European Communities, 1945–72', by F. S. Northedge (Section 2 of this unit).
2 'Time-lags in Political Psychology', by Uwe Kitzinger (Section 3 of this unit and Reader pp. 7–22.)
3 'The Historical Development of the European Communities', by Roy Pryce (Section 4 of this unit).

'Britain and the European Communities, 1945–72' by F. S. Northedge (Section 2 of this unit) examines the developing relationship between Britain and Europe in the years since the Second World War. It is a specific historical focus on the reasons for the change in the attitude of the British Government and public towards unification during these years. The author advances the view that Britain had little choice but to join the Communities. The decision was largely determined for her.

The article in the Reader 'Time-lags in Political Psychology' (pp. 7–22) by Uwe Kitzinger covers some of the same ground as Northedge. Kitzinger too has a thesis to advance, that there has been a 'time-lag' between membership of the European Communities being in Britain's interest, and recognition of that fact by Government and public. In so doing he raises issues far wider than those relating to just the EEC.

Roy Pryce's article 'The Historical Development of the European Communities' (Section 4 of this unit) summarizes the history of Europe since 1945. It charts in more general terms the steps towards the foundation of the European Communities, examines the motives behind the movement, and plots the growth and expansion of the Communities since 1958.

These three papers are intended to give you an understanding of the progress towards European unity and provide an historical background to the rest of the course.

We have set each of the essential readings into a context consisting of introductions, activities and questions. These have been designed to help you to learn and to draw out the major points of the articles. If you wish, you may read the articles independently of these comments and activities.

The activities take several forms, some are self-test questions which will help you to check your own progress; others call for summaries of particular issues when, if need be, you can refer back to a section of the reading; and finally, some call for evaluations which are subjective and for which there is no precise answer.

Do as many of the activities as you can. If you run short of time choose those which are most relevant to your interests.

Recommended reading

These readings are all to be found in the Reader. They contain further information on the matters dealt with in the essential readings. Although the CMA does not test your knowledge of the recommended readings, some of the activities do involve reference to them.

1 ' "With" them but not "of" them: Brief Extracts from British Politicians' Views on Britain's Relations with Europe, 1946–61.' (Reader, pp. 23–8).

2 'The Great Debate: Extracts from the Commons Debate on Entry of October 1971' (Reader, pp. 29–42).

3 Patrick O'Donovan, 'Who do we think we are?' (Reader, pp. 42–5).

Reference reading

These readings should be used to locate specific information or to answer particular questions as they arise. The chronology is found both in the unit and in the Reader, the other two in the unit (Section 6).

1 Chronology of events in the formation of the European Communities.

2 A Glossary of Western European Organizations.

3 The Communiqué of the Paris Summit, October 1972.

Preliminary questions

Before you read the unit try to answer the following questions. They are designed simply so that you can test your factual knowledge. *Work quickly through the questions, and do not spend time pondering over them.* Do not worry if you are unable to answer them at this stage. If you are able to complete all or most of the questions correctly it does not mean that the unit has nothing to offer you. These are factual questions while the unit is also concerned with the analysis of ideas, attitudes and motives.

1   The following initials stand for European organizations. Name the organization and say very briefly what it does:

   a NATO
   b EEC
   c EFTA
   d Euratom
   e WEU
   f ECSC
   g OECD

2   What do these initials stand for:

   a CAP
   b GATT

3   The following statesmen are among those who have played an important role in the development of the European Communities. Write two or three sentences identifying them and their work for European unity.

   a Robert Schuman
   b Jean Monnet
   c Konrad Adenauer
   d Walter Hallstein
   e Reginald Maudling
   f Paul-Henri Spaak

4   Organize the following into a chronological order and if possible give dates:

   a the Davignon Report
   b the founding of the Coal and Steel Community
   c the Paris Summit
   d the first British application for membership
   e the signing of the Rome Treaty
   f the completion of the customs union
   g the formation of EFTA
   h the Luxembourg Compromise

5   In January and February 1970 the Directorate-General of Press and Information carried out an opinion survey in the then six members of the European Communities, and Britain. This was published in a preliminary report 'Les Européens: Oui à l'Europe' (Europeans say 'Yes to Europe'). Set out below are five of the questions which were asked. If you had been selected as part of the survey sample, how would you have answered the questions – For; Against; Don't Know?

How would you answer now?

a   Are you in favour of, or against, Britain joining the European Common Market?

In favour: Against: Don't know:

b   Assuming that Britain did join, would you be for or against the evolution of the Common Market towards the political formation of a United States of Europe?

For: Against: Don't know:

c   Would you be in favour of, or against, the election of a European Parliament by direct universal suffrage; that is a Parliament elected by all the voters in the member countries?

In favour: Against: Don't know:

d   Would you be willing to accept, over and above your own government, a European Government responsible for a common policy in foreign affairs, defence and the economy?

Willing: Not willing: Don't know:

e   If a President of a United States of Europe were being elected by popular vote, would you be willing to vote for a candidate not of your own country – if his personality and programme corresponded more closely to your ideas than those of the candidates of your own country?

Willing: Not willing: Don't know:

The results of this poll are discussed by Uwe Kitzinger in 'Time-lags in Political Psychology' (Reader, pp. 21–2: Essential Reading). Compare your answers with those obtained from analysis of the original questionnaires.

Europe and You.

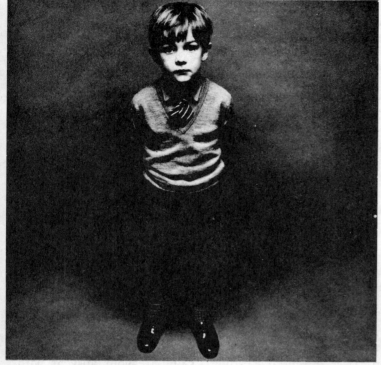

European Movement
We've got to get in to get on.

Give him cheap butter-now and let him worry
about where his bread is coming from later.

In 1958, when the Common Market was started, we in Britain were enjoying higher living standards than the people of Europe.

Today we have a lower income per head than any Common Market country except Italy.

For the last thirteen years, the economies of the Common Market countries have been growing at twice the rate of ours.

In fact, they're still doing it.

If things go on like this, by 1980 we stand a good chance of being one of the poorest countries in Europe.

Not much of a future for our children. Unless we give them the same opportunities as their European counterparts.

It's true that if we join the Common Market the price of food will go up.

But the extra cost on household budgets will only be something like one penny in the pound per year, spaced over five years.

So think about it.

We can foot that bill now. Or leave our children to pay a much bigger price in the future.

European Movement
We've got to get in to get on.

Published by the European Movement, 78 Chandos House, Buckingham Gate, London, S.W.1. Printed by Waterlow and Sons Limited

The Common Market.

By now you must be tired of waffle and ready for the facts.

1. Who is in the Common Market now?

The six members of the Common Market who signed the Treaty of Rome in March, 1957, are Belgium, France, Holland, Italy, Luxembourg and West Germany.

2. Who would be in the enlarged Market?

If the applications are successful the Common Market will consist of the six original members and Britain, Denmark, Ireland and Norway.

3. What is the point of the Common Market?

Economically—to provide the large, dynamic, home market needed for economic growth. But the Market also has wider social aims. A fundamental one, laid down in the Treaty of Rome, is '. . . the constant improvement of the living and working conditions of their peoples.' Another is '. . . to strengthen the unity of their economies and to ensure their harmonious development by reducing the disparities between the various regions and mitigating the backwardness of the less favoured ones.'

4. Will it work?

It already is working. Just compare the rise in real wages during the first 10 years of the Common Market. The economies of Common Market countries have been expanding at double the rate of Britain since 1958.

5. How will it affect my wages?

In 1958 the average wage in Britain was £2 a week more than the average in the Common Market. By 1970 it was £5 a week less. You can draw your own conclusions from that.

6. Will the cost of living go up?

Yes. There's no way of avoiding it. The cost of joining the Common Market will be something like a 5% rise in the cost of living. But that will be spread over the first 5 year transition period, working out at a penny in the pound on household budgets.

Which is certainly nothing like some of the alarming prophecies that have been made. Although the cost of living will rise, so will wages—so the standard of living will also increase.

7. What about holidays?

In Britain we average 17-21 days paid holiday per year. The Common Market countries average 27-35 days paid holiday per year.

8. What will happen to our standard of living?

It will go up. In the first ten years of the Common Market, the standard of living (the measurement of real wages after allowing for rising prices) increased by 75% in Holland. Even the lowest rise, in France, was a healthy 41%. In the same period the standard of living in Britain rose only 20%.

Joining the Market will make possible a faster improvement in the living standards of the British people.

9. Won't it mean the end of the Welfare State, the National Health Service and in particular help for the Old People?

Photo courtesy of the Embassy of the Federal German Republic.

Old Age Pensioners enjoy greater benefits in the Common Market.

No. Every Common Market country spends more per person on Social Welfare than Britain. In every Common Market country, family allowances and pensions are higher than they are in Britain. And, every Common Market country spends more per person on housing than Britain.

10. What will happen to our independence of action in the world?

Complete independence of countries like ours is, in this day and age, an illusion. But, by sharing, as a right, in European decisions we can begin to defend and protect British national interests effectively once more.

11. What will happen to our civil rights?

As national parliaments will continue to exercise their sovereign powers in most areas of policy (except those delegated by unanimous consent to European institutions) all our traditional rights and liberties—the right to trial by jury, for instance; the presumption of innocence, etc.—will still remain unchanged.

12. Will we lose our national character and identity?

Well, it doesn't seem to have happened to any of the present members and, unless you believe

Photo courtesy of the Italian State Tourist Office.

Italian girls get between 29 and 47 days' paid holiday each year—compared to our 17 to 21 days.

that our national character is weaker than theirs, there's no reason to believe that it will happen to us.

13. What will happen to the Royal Family?

The Queen will continue as constitutional Monarch. The Common Market already has three members who are monarchies and their Sovereigns' status has not been affected. In fact, if the present applications succeed the enlarged Common Market will contain ten countries and six monarchies.

14. What about the Commonwealth and our other friends in the world?

Britain will be the centre of a chain linking them with the enlarged community. They will benefit from closer relationship not only with a strengthened Britain, but with the whole of the community.

15. What has Britain to offer the Common Market?

Unrivalled experience in world affairs; long established democratic institutions and traditions; advanced technology and the greatest industrial potential of any European country—all these should help us make a really important contribution to expanding the Common Market. And through the Common Market to a powerful place in world affairs.

16. What has the Common Market to offer us?

No other country depends so heavily for its livelihood on what it can sell abroad, as Britain. Yet we are the only major industrial nation in the world which does not enjoy a home market of at least 100 million people. Which is why we are so vulnerable economically.

The enlarged Common Market will have a total population of about 270 million people. (Larger than the U.S.A.'s 204 million or Russia's 235 million.) Membership of this community with its immense economic resources would bring us greater economic prosperity at home and greater influence in the world. And, most important, give our children a greater stake in the future.

Section 2
Britain and the European Communities 1945-72

Contents

F S Northedge Professor of International Relations in the University of London. Read for Classical Moderations at Merton College, Oxford, 1937–9, lectured to HM Forces in the Second World War, passed BSc (Economics) with First in 1948 at the London School of Economics. Joined the International Relations Department at the LSE in 1949, received PhD degree in 1953 and served as Convenor of Department from January 1969 until December 1972. Has written two standard works on British foreign policy from 1916 to 1939 and 1945 to 1961 and other books on different aspects of international relations. A frequent broadcaster. Has previously contributed to Open University courses on decision-making.

Course team introduction

Although the United Kingdom has always had strong links with Western Europe, joining the EEC has been a conscious act of political will committing this country to a formal relationship and formal commitments to the other members of the Community. This has many implications for the future.

In the past Britain has also had many and varied interests around the world, do these now take second place to the new European commitment? Does this commitment necessarily mean that Britain is now primarily a European, as opposed to a world power? Can Britain still claim the position of special independence and objectivity – the honest broker role – which some have claimed for her in the past? These are some questions raised by British membership of the European Communities, but do not expect precise answers for these are the imponderables of a developing situation. They are posed rhetorically to challenge you to consider the global implications of the enlarged Community.

This paper examines the British Government's attitude and policies towards Europe in detail. Apart from the chronological treatment of the major events, the author presents a clear interpretation of the reasons why Britain joined the European Communities.

This interpretation tends towards 'determinism' – that is an interpretation which regards the actual sequence of events as being more or less inevitable. As you read through the paper note in the margin where the author explains how the possible alternative policies for Britain were gradually narrowed down until, in his opinion, the only course of action remaining was membership of the EEC.

Britain and the European Communities, 1945–72

F. S. Northedge

It is often said that the British people have a traditional attitude of detachment from Europe and hostility to the whole idea of European unity. This is reflected in many disparaging British sayings about Europe: 'the wogs begin at Calais' and so on. But these attitudes are in fact comparatively recent; they date from the acquisition of the British Empire and the preoccupation of the British with imperial problems, say from the beginning of the nineteenth century. Before that Britain was deeply involved in Europe; in the early eighteenth century the Duke of Marlborough led a European army to victory in the heart of Austria and as late as 1815 a British Foreign Secretary, Lord Castlereagh, almost succeeded in taking Britain into a permanent arrangement for European political consultation. So there is some sense in saying that Britain, having decolonized her Empire, is returning to an original European role.

1
Britain's traditional attitude towards European union

1

With a vast overseas Empire British governments before 1939 had based their national security on a number of devices including the balance of power.[1] This did not encourage them to look kindly on the idea of European unity. Moreover, the two world wars, which might have worked to strengthen the case for British participation in the movement towards European unity, actually had reverse effects. After 1918 Britain was preoccupied with such problems as the co-ordination of policies in the self-governing Dominions of the Empire and naval rivalry with the United States. After 1945 there was the dominating question of the need to harmonize relations between the United States and the Soviet Union and to maintain a hearing for British and European interests at the Super-Power level.

2

[1] 'Balance of power' generally means a method of maintaining the independence of state-members of the international system by forming a coalition of states against the strongest and most threatening power of the day.

2
British attitudes towards schemes for strengthening European bonds before 1945

Hence there was, even before the Second World War, a consistent record of British coldness towards schemes for tying more closely together the European states in the twentieth century. The embodiment of this attitude in British foreign policy can be seen, first, in British opposition to the creation of a Supreme Allied Command in the First World War. Even after the Allied disaster on the Somme in 1917 the British government was suspicious at the idea of placing British forces under a common Allied Commander, all the more so because in the nature of the situation he had to be French. Similarly, there was no support in Britain for the French proposal at the Paris Peace Conference in 1919 that the new League of Nations, itself an essentially European organization, should dispose of united military and naval forces. **3**

The same pattern was continued in the early 1920s when Britain rejected plans for the closer integration of the League of Nations such as the Draft Treaty of Mutual Assistance and the Geneva Protocol for the Peaceful Settlement of International Disputes. As before, the refusal to lose control of British armed forces, especially the navy, and the alleged needs of the Empire, played important roles in this policy. In 1925, at the Locarno Conference, Britain did undertake a specific commitment in Europe, but this was confined to the guarantee of two frontiers and, even so, military staff talks to implement it were never mounted. In 1930 Britain was instrumental in securing the rejection of a plan for European union put forward by the French Prime Minister, Aristide Briand, the Foreign Office calling it 'vague and puzzling idealism'. **4**

Ten years later, when France was undergoing military defeat at the hands of Nazi Germany, Winston Churchill, the British Prime Minister, made a desperate offer of the political union of Britain and France. But by his own account, all his instincts were against it when it was first proposed and he only agreed to it as a morale booster to keep the French army in the field. This offer is unique of all the proposals between 1914 and 1945 in that it came from London, not Paris. British attitudes towards European union in the twentieth century must always be considered against the background of persistently stormy Anglo-French relations. **5**

3
The British position at the end of the Second World War

General de Gaulle, who was to prove such a firm antagonist of British entry into the European Communities in the 1960s, held as one of his strongest anathemas the Yalta Conference of February 1945 at which, according to him, Europe was divided into American and Soviet hegemonies, this being later confirmed at the Potsdam Conference of July-August 1945. The fact that Britain, alone of all the European states outside Russia, was represented at those two conferences not only made them all the more obnoxious to de Gaulle; it also made British politicians think they had a special role, in defending European interests in the inner conclaves of the great Powers. **6**

Britain had retained her sovereignty during the Second World War and the continental states had not; either their sovereignty had been taken over by the Axis Powers during the war or, as enemies, they lost their sovereignty to the Allies at the end of the war. This, together with the unitary character of the British state, gave the British a peculiarly protective attitude towards their own sovereignty in the years after 1945. **7**

The economic problems of reconstruction in 1945 had the effect of turning British attention towards the United States, whose economic strength seemed if anything to be enhanced by the war. America was the home of the dollar, the scarcest of the world's currencies in the immediate post-war years: Britain first contracted a dollar loan worth £1,000 million in December 1945, which was quickly exhausted, and then grasped at the offer of massive American aid for Europe known as the Marshall Plan which covered the period 1948–52. During the Marshall Plan Britain came nearer than ever before to co-operation with her European neighbours; at the same time the **8**

16

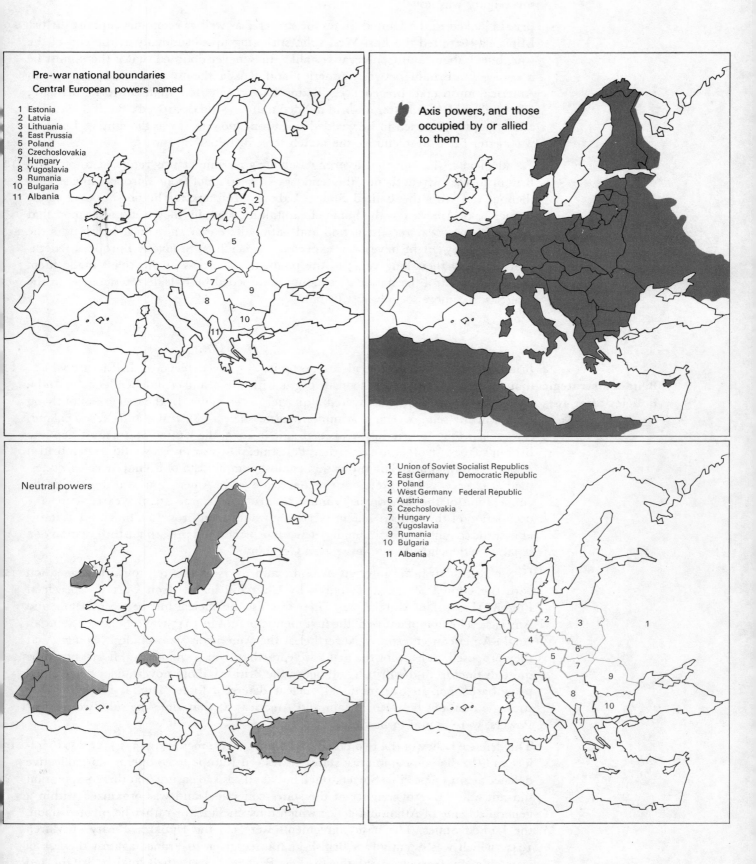

Pre-war national boundaries
Central European powers named

1 Estonia
2 Latvia
3 Lithuania
4 East Prussia
5 Poland
6 Czechoslovakia
7 Hungary
8 Yugoslavia
9 Rumania
10 Bulgaria
11 Albania

Axis powers, and those
occupied by or allied
to them

Neutral powers

1 Union of Soviet Socialist Republics
2 East Germany   Democratic Republic
3 Poland
4 West Germany   Federal Republic
5 Austria
6 Czechoslovakia
7 Hungary
8 Yugoslavia
9 Rumania
10 Bulgaria

11 Albania

Plan allowed the British to determine the limits of their co-operation with western Europe – traditional international co-operation was welcome, any notion of merging sovereignty was not.

Britain looked to the United States for strategic as well as economic support. British Ministers regretted the East-West split, springing up so suddenly at the end of the war, but, Labour and Conservatives alike, they never doubted that if there must be a choice for Britain between America and Russia the 'special relationship' with America must take precedence. 'Better a world united than a world divided', Churchill said, 'but better a world divided than a world destroyed'. But if it was vital after 1945 for America to be wedded to Europe, no one, it was thought, in London, was better fitted to solemnize the match than Britain. 9

Paradoxically, the fact that a strong Labour government was returned to office in Britain in 1945 strengthened the tendency to keep aloof from Europe while strengthening ties with the United States. Labour Ministers might be supposed to be suspicious of America as the home of capitalism: actually they well understood that for British post-war reconstruction and national security they must look across the Atlantic. They might have been expected, as socialists, to favour European federation; actually their long years in the political wilderness in the 1930s made them anxious to control the national economy unimpeded by outside interference, in the interests of a more socially just Britain. 10

**4
Britain's strategic
policies after 1945**

Britain in 1945 had technical responsibility for the defence of an Empire which, though decolonization was soon to begin with the grant of independence to India and Pakistan in 1947, still covered a quarter of the globe. In the defence of outlying sectors of the self-governing Commonwealth, such as Australia and New Zealand, it was clear that, in Britain's weakened state in 1945, the United States must step into Britain's shoes. In other areas, such as Palestine, post-war unrest would stretch British resources to the limit. The protection against communism of friendly weaker states, such as Greece and Turkey, must be handed over to America, as was done with the enunciation of the American Truman Doctrine in March 1947. Nearer home the occupation of the British zone in Germany would soon prove too much for Britain; at first she sought American financial assistance and then pressed for the creation of a separate independent state in western Germany. 11

Hence British strategic interests at home and overseas pointed towards association with the United States, as favoured by Churchill in his 'Iron Curtain' speech at Fulton, Missouri, in March 1946. There was also the nuclear link between Britain and America. The manufacture of the first atomic bombs in 1945 was to a large extent an Anglo-American enterprise. Nevertheless the Americans soon made it evident that they proposed, at least for the first few years, that their own nuclear efforts should be quite distinct from the British and hence the British Labour government determined to embark upon its own national nuclear deterrent force. Thus it was clear that strategic relations between Britain and America, at that time the sole two nuclear Powers, were bound to be close. 12

The defence policy of the two post-war Labour governments (1945–1951) was therefore to help the non-communist states in western Europe to co-operate for collective defence against a possible Soviet attack but at all costs to ensure that this co-operation did not affect the sovereignty of the states concerned and was organized within a general scheme of Atlantic defence which must include, or rather be pivoted upon, the United States. The basic agreements were (1) the Dunkirk Treaty of March 1947, which was essentially a British guarantee given to France against the risk of aggression by Germany; (2) the Brussels Pact of March 1948 linking Britain and France with the Benelux States (Belgium, Luxembourg, the Netherlands) in collective 13

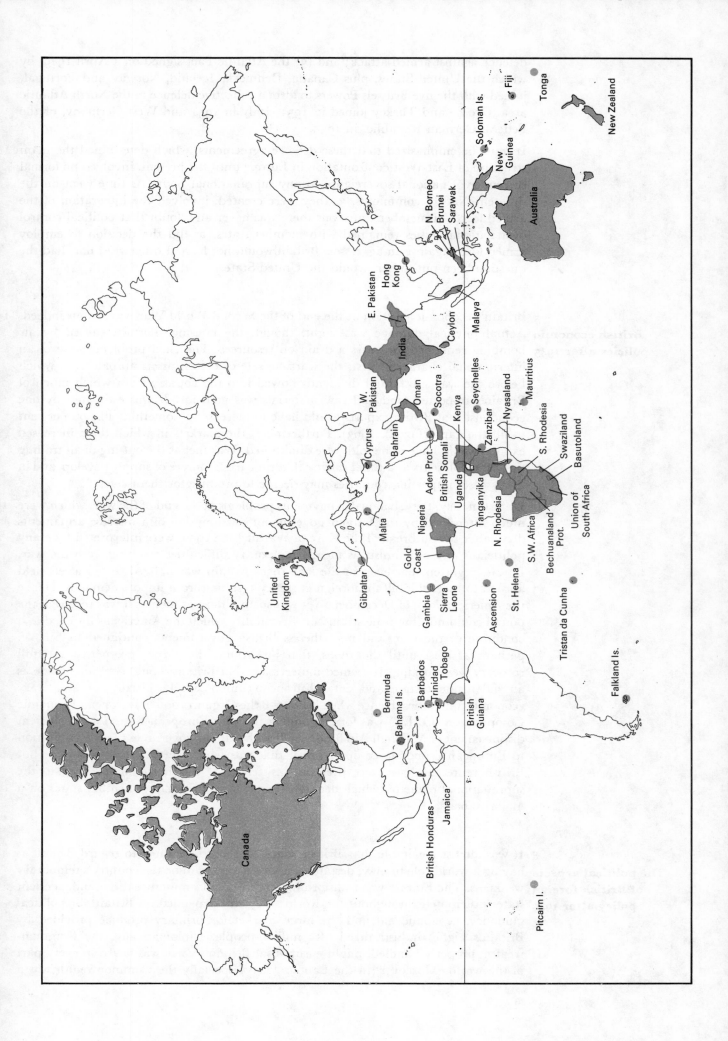

New Zealand

Tonga

Fiji

Soloman Is.

New Guinea

Australia

N. Borneo
Brunei
Sarawak

Hong Kong

E. Pakistan

Malaya

Ceylon

India

W. Pakistan

Oman

Socotra

Kenya

Seychelles

Mauritius

Nyasaland

S. Rhodesia

Zanzibar

Swaziland

Basutoland

Bahrain

Cyprus

Aden Prot.

British Somali

Uganda

Tanganyika

N. Rhodesia

Union of
South Africa

S.W. Africa

Bechuanaland
Prot.

Malta

Nigeria

Gold
Coast

Gibraltar

United
Kingdom

Gambia

Sierra
Leone

Ascension

St. Helena

Tristan da Cunha

Falkland Is.

Bermuda

Barbados

Trinidad

Tobago

British
Guiana

Bahama Is.

British Honduras

Jamaica

Canada

Pitcairn I.

defence against armed attack; and (3) the Atlantic Pact signed on 4 April 1949, by which the United States, plus Canada, Denmark, Iceland, Norway and Portugal, joined with the five Brussels Powers to form a collective defence in the North Atlantic area. Greece and Turkey joined in 1951, Italy in 1954 and West Germany, or the Federal German Republic, in 1955.

It must be emphasized that these defence agreements, which determined the main 14 structure of East-West confrontation in Europe until the present, involved no formal surrender of national sovereignty to any supranational body. As time went on the different NATO commands, as they were created, involved the integration of the armed forces of member states but there was never any doubt that political control over national forces remained with member states, as did the decision to employ armed force against an aggressor. Britain would not have it otherwise; nor, had the question been put to her, would the United States.

5 British economic policies after 1945

Britain's economic position at the end of the Second World War was serious indeed. 15 Actual physical damage was slight, though the housing shortage caused by air bombing remained for years a drain on resources. The chief problems were of an international character: first, the wartime sale of British assets abroad from which before the war substantial dividends flowed into the country from which much of Britain's imported food and raw materials was paid for. It was estimated by one economist that British exports would have to increase by something like 66 per cent to fill the gap (Harrod, 1963). Furthermore, the markets in which these increased exports would have to be sold were diminished. War means the cutting of all trading ties, often for years at a time; during that time fresh sources of supply develop, and in many cases importing countries may decide to produce for themselves.

Unfortunately, these balance of payments problems at the end of the war, which were 16 much intensified by the Labour government's assumption of a massive armaments drive after the outbreak of the Korean War in June 1950, were interpreted by many politicians and economists as merely temporary difficulties resulting from the war. It was forgotten that even in the late 1930s Britain was obliged to sell assets held abroad to meet the bill for foreign currency resulting from import demands. Hence the American loan of December 1945 was spent almost as soon as it was received, the pound could not stand the strain of convertibility which the Americans imposed as a condition of the loan and nevertheless British governments continued to believe, perhaps at least until the 1960s, that just round the corner prosperity and full recovery were lurking. It seemed unnecessary that Britain should commit suicide as an independent state and enter European union simply because of temporary economic difficulties. Hence when in 1947–8 the Organization of European Economic Co-operation (OEEC) was formed among the west European states for the efficient disbursement of Marshall Aid funds the British Labour government had no objection to European economic co-operation if that was what the Americans wanted; but British representatives were tirelessly insistent that this must not proceed to the supranational plane on which decisions might be made among member states on a majority basis.

6 The political aspects of British foreign policy after 1945

It was almost inevitable that British ministers should continue to regard Britain as 17 having a world role to play, despite what was assumed to be the country's temporary weakness. The Empire was transforming itself into a Commonwealth of independent states distributed throughout the world; they still depended on Britain for political guidance, economic aid and the large market for primary produce provided by Britain's highly industrialized fifty million people. Diplomatically, the Commonwealth, properly handled, might ensure that Britain's voice was heard in every part of the world. Moreover, in the Labour Party especially the Commonwealth was a much more powerful symbol than Europe; the poverty and backwardness of the ex-colonies were regarded as a challenge by equalitarian Labour leaders, and the multiracial Commonwealth seemed a crucible in which racial equality could be forged more effectively than in the more formal United Nations. Whenever Labour leaders had a choice between the Commonwealth and Europe it was the former which invariably seemed more congenial to them.

The other area in which Britain seemed to have a role of political leadership was 18 the United States. Although, as we have seen, Britain and Europe after 1945 were, in British eyes, desperately dependent on the United States for economic recovery and military defence, there was a sense in which America was perhaps equally dependent on Britain, and that was for political and diplomatic tutelage. At one stage, say between the end of the war and the announcement of the Truman Doctrine in March 1947, the American giant needed to be alerted to the dangers of Soviet dominance of the whole of Europe when its strongest inclination was to retire into the comforts of the American life. Once engaged in the defence of the democratic world, the Americans tended to fly to the other extreme and dedicate themselves to unrelenting struggle against communism at almost any price. On two crucial occasions, in November 1950 and again in 1954, British governments felt they had a duty to act as a restraint on the United States. In 1950 this was to strengthen the more moderate voices in America which did not wish to provoke Communist China into entering the Korean War; in 1954 it was Britain's responsibility to press the Americans to work for a peaceful solution of the crisis in South East Asia resulting from the collapse of French resistance to communist forces at the siege of Dien Bien Phu in Vietnam.

Throughout the post-war period up until about 1960 British ministers felt they had a 19 vital part to play, in standing as a conciliator between the two Super-Powers, while being firmly committed to the western alliance, in urging on both Powers tension-easing agreements such as the Partial Nuclear Test Ban Agreement of 1963, in suggesting schemes of arms control in Central Europe to lessen the risks of collision. It may be agreed that these mediatory functions could have been just as well performed by a Britain working in close accord with her European partners but this is not how British ministers saw it. For them, a world role for Britain was natural in the light of her history and experience, and it demanded interventions at the highest realm of world politics in order to better East-West relations. And to work for peace, in which Britain had the strongest possible interest, required her presence at the 'top table' as long as that position could be maintained.

The Western Leaders at the ill-fated Paris Summit in 1960   From left to right: Harold Macmillan, Prime Minister of the United Kingdom; Dwight D Eisenhower, President of the USA; Charles de Gaulle, President of France; Konrad Adenauer, Chancellor of the Federal Republic of Germany

7
British attitudes towards European integration proposals

The official British attitude to European Union in the ten years or so following 20 1945 was that the federalists in western Europe should not be encouraged and that the federal movement would no doubt blow itself out in time, leaving the way open to strictly intergovernmental co-operation in limited fields, especially economics and defence; but that if the European federalists pressed on with their visionary schemes, Britain did not object to a loose form of 'association' with any organization resulting from their efforts but would go no further.

The first really overt sign of the Labour government's attitude came with the 21 negotiation of the Statute of the Council of Europe in 1949. The Council was to be a two-chamber body set up by intergovernmental agreement, one chamber being a Consultative Assembly consisting of Members of Parliament of the participating states (which were limited to non-communist northern and western Europe), and the other being a Committee of Ministers of member states. It is questionable whether, at this early stage of European integration, west European governments were ready for the surrender of 'real but limited powers' which the proponents of the Council of Europe were asking for. But that question did not need to be raised in view of the adamant refusal of the British Foreign Secretary, Mr Ernest Bevin, to see the Council's Statute shaped in the way desired by the federalists. Bevin's distaste for the idea of any really effective Council of Europe is reflected in his immediate reaction to the proposal, when he exploded, 'once you open that Pandora's box, you'll find it full of Trojan horses'. It was Ernest Bevin who, more than anyone else, ensured that in the Council, which began to exist in May 1949, the Consultative Assembly should be firmly subordinate to the Committee of Ministers, which was to control the purse strings of the new body and the agenda of the Consultative Assembly; that the Council should not deal with defence, which was by now firmly in the hands of the traditionally international Brussels Treaty Organization and the Atlantic Alliance; and that states adhering to the Statute of the Council of Europe would be signing away none of their sovereign powers.

European unionists, thus having been foiled on the federal front, then fell back on 22 another approach. Since the British Labour government was quite firm against any overall surrender of sovereignty to a federal executive and legislature in western Europe, how would it react to the idea of functional organizations, that is, organs linking together specific activities in the different states and gradually assuming the powers of the various national governments over these activities? After all, the British government, in rejecting federal proposals such as the Council of Europe, was evidently not averse to functional co-operation provided always that it was based on intergovernmental agreement and maintained the individual state's right to say 'no' to any specific proposal.

Accordingly, in June 1950, the French Foreign Minister, Robert Schuman, proposed 23 to the west European states a functional plan, to which he gave his name, for bringing under a single control the coal and steel industries of western Europe. The new organization, later known as the European Coal and Steel Community (ECSC), was to be supranational in two respects: when the Community was fully in being, its executive organ, the High Authority, would adopt its resolutions on the basis of majority voting, which meant that any member state could be bound without its consent; and, secondly, the decisions of the High Authority should be directly binding upon people and organizations without their governments being involved.

European states which were notified about the Schuman plan by the French 24 authorities were asked to send representatives to a Paris conference to embody the Schuman principles into a treaty but only if they accepted the principle of supra-nationality first. On the basis of objection to this condition the British Labour government refused to attend the Paris conference, at which six other west European states – the Benelux countries, France, Italy and Western Germany – agreed to the pooling of their coal and steel industries under the control of a single High Authority.

The ECSC came into being without Britain in 1952. It was the first definite parting of the ways between Britain and the countries known thereafter as the Six.

In the British Parliament the Conservative Opposition, under Churchill's leader- 25 ship, severely criticized the Labour government for letting slip the opportunity created by the Schuman plan, but when the Conservatives themselves were returned to office in October 1951 they showed no more liking for the principle of supranation- ality. This was strikingly shown in 1952 when the French Government, this time in the person of René Pleven, the Defence Minister, came out with a second and more far-reaching plan for functional integration. This sprang from American pressure for the rearmament of Western Germany which arose in its turn from fears of a com- munist offensive against western Europe to accompany the aggression of Communist North Korea against South Korea which began in June 1950. The idea of West German rearmament was naturally abhorrent to the French, to say nothing of Britain, the Low Countries and Scandinavia; the solution to the dilemma proposed by the French was the creation of a supranational European Defence Community (EDC) to take command of the armed forces of participating states, including the proposed new forces of Western Germany.

Steaming towards unity! A beflagged train celebrates the opening of Europe's first common market — for coal. 10 February 1953.

To pool heavy industries under a single authority was one thing; to create a 26 supranational army in western Europe was quite another. It necessitated an inter- national cabinet to direct the force and at this point the notions of federalism and functionalism met and were fused together (see Barber, Unit 4). But if Britain could not stomach a supranational functional organ, she certainly could not accept a federal organ. And so it proved. Churchill, who had warmed to the idea of a European army, decisively rejected the notion of British participation and it was partly on this ground that the French Chamber of Deputies declined to ratify the EDC in August 1954, leading to its demise.

It is testimony, however, to the strength and resilience of the European Union 27
movement that almost at once after the failure of EDC the movement took another
step in the direction of complete political unification by attempting to create a single
economic community (the EEC) among the original Six. At the Messina Conference
in Sicily in 1955, with Britain now present only in the person of an observer, the
main outlines of the EEC were laid down. It is characteristic of the perennial
British preoccupation with international trade that the EEC, which was finally
embodied in a treaty signed in Rome by the Six two years later, is generally known
in Britain (as it is also often known on the Continent) as the 'Common Market',
that is a free trade area between the participating states and a single and uniform
tariff between them all and the rest of the world. In fact, of course, the Rome
Treaty makes evident that something more far-reaching is sought: that is, the unification under the control of a single set of institutions of the economic systems, practice and law of the contributing states, the institution of amalgamated welfare and
social services, the standardization of legislation governing trade and commerce,
labour, transport, wholesale and retail trade, and of policies for dealing with other
countries including the developing nations. In fact, the EEC when fully mature
would replace the six national economic systems of the member states by one
amalgamated economy, to be regarded as the basis for political unification in western
Europe.[2] The comprehensiveness of European Union as envisaged by the Rome
Treaty signatories is reflected in the fact that the institutions of the three Communities – the original ECSC, the EEC and Euratom, the agency created along
with EEC for co-operation between the Six in the field of nuclear development –
would be (and have now been) fused together to form one executive, legislative
and judicial structure.

The Rome Treaty faced Britain with her greatest challenge on the whole issue of 28
European unification. The comprehensiveness of the integration envisaged by the
EEC meant that if it succeeded western Europe, or at least the Six, would not be
far from political unification within, say, a quarter of a century. A historical object
of British policy, the division of the Continent or at least its unification under
British leadership, would be frustrated, and Britain, to whom was due to a large
extent the survival of Europe in 1945, would be dangerously isolated. Moreover,
the implementation of the Rome Treaty, if only in the form of a customs union
among the Six, must have the effect of dividing non-communist Europe into at least
two commercial areas, and to this Britain, with her heavy stake in international
trade, could not be indifferent.

Nevertheless, on at least two counts there were seemingly insurmountable objections 29
to Britain joining the Six. On the one hand, as before, the supranational principle
embraced by the Six stuck in Britain's throat. On the other, Britain could hardly
accept a common tariff and financial policy for agriculture. To do so meant not
only to abandon trading preferences for Commonwealth food imports – cheese and
butter from New Zealand, wheat from Canada and Australia, cane sugar from the
West Indies, cocoa and such like from Africa – which Britain had granted since
1932; it meant to erect tariff barriers *against* such imports. It also meant to exchange
a cheap food policy which Britain ensured through subsidizing the farmer directly,
for the Continental dear food policy which the Six practised by allowing the farmer
to charge market prices for his produce supplemented by intervention payments
from EEC funds when market prices fell below a certain level.

Consequently, during 1958 Britain tried in negotiations conducted on the British side 30
by Mr Reginald Maudling to persuade the Six to place the EEC within a wider free
trade area restricted to industrial goods. There would, after a suitable transitional
period, be no tariffs on industrial goods between the EEC as a unit and other

[2]Such developments may have been envisaged by some, but the Treaty of Rome does not provide the basis for
all such amalgamation – hence the negotiations on economic and monetary union. (Ed.)

members of the free trade area, nor between the latter themselves. The EEC states would retain their single tariff with the rest of the world and other member states of the free trade area would maintain what tariff each saw fit on its trade with the rest of the world.

Technical difficulties of operating the Maudling scheme apart, it was clear that the supranational principle had become a bedrock issue between Britain and the Six: either Britain must concede and accept it or she and the Six must go their separate ways. France spoke for the Six when the Gaullist Minister of Information, Jacques Sustelle, announced the end of the Maudling talks in November 1958. Britain went ahead with six other like-minded west European states – Austria, Denmark, Norway, Sweden and Switzerland, later joined by Portugal – to form the European Free Trade Association (EFTA) based on the Maudling principles. But it was generally recognized among its member states that the purpose of EFTA, based on a Stockholm convention signed on 4 January 1960, was less to provide an alternative to the EEC than to keep its member states together while they were negotiating suitable terms of entry into the EEC. 31

René Pleven. When French Defence Minister he proposed a far-reaching plan for functional integration

– **Reginald Maudling tried to persuade the Six to place the EEC within a wider free-trade area**

8
The British change of direction, 1961

Nineteen months after the signing of the Stockholm convention came the momentous decision of Mr Harold Macmillan, who had succeeded Sir Anthony Eden as Prime Minister in January 1957, to open negotiations with the Six with a view to submitting an application for membership of the EEC if suitable terms could be agreed. As far as Britain was concerned, the conditions the Macmillan Government was insisting upon were three: that the interests of British agriculture and of the Commonwealth must be safeguarded and that there must be suitable provision for the EFTA states. 32

The circumstances which had brought the Conservative government round to this position from its very different stance during the Maudling negotiations were obvious enough. First, it had become clear that the drive towards European integration was no mere pipe dream which would be dissipated when hard practical difficulties were encountered; by now too many interests in western Europe were tied up with the movement towards integration to allow it to fail. 'We are condemned to succeed', said one Belgian diplomat. British politicians had been inclined to write off these schemes of integration as idle Continental talk. Now a different language was necessary. 33

Secondly, the serious consequences for Britain of non-communist Europe being 34 divided into two separate trading blocs were making themselves evident. The Commonwealth was bound to be of declining importance as a market for the high-quality manufactured goods in which Britain must now specialize; much of the Commonwealth, especially the newly decolonized countries, had low purchasing power until such time as their economic 'take-off' occurred; nor could the six EFTA countries, with their relatively small population, really be expected to provide a substitute for the EEC for British goods. The EEC market for British exports was still small compared with the Commonwealth but it was increasing more rapidly, especially in the more sophisticated export lines where Britain's future lay.

Ernest Bevin, Foreign Secretary of the United Kingdom, signing the Statute of the Council of Europe

Thirdly, the 'stop-go' pattern of the British economy seemed to be becoming 35 permanent. After a few months of booming activity, though with low productivity and rising prices, the authorities had to apply the brake in order to reduce pressure on the balance of payments. With another burst of activity following such a 'squeeze', the process was reproduced over and over again. The basic reason for this was that if productivity was to be raised and 'overheating' of the economy avoided, new investment was essential to replace Britain's ageing capital equipment. But this, as always, raised prices, with consequent adverse effects on the country's financial account with the rest of the world. Investment had to be slowed down, then speeded up and the cycle renewed again. Conservative ministers began to think that by plunging Britain into the highly competitive EEC they would give industrialists and exporters a 'douche of cold water' sufficient to lift them out of the lethargy which made this vicious circle possible.

Fourthly, in the years since the ECSC Britain's international position had changed 36 for the worse. In 1956 Britain had tried, with France, to mount a not especially difficult military operation in Egypt and had failed miserably. Could a state which could bungle a modest affair so badly really be considered a world power? In 1960 Britain had had to accept the failure of the home-bred missile 'Blue Streak'; at the same time the US had discontinued the manufacture of the 'Skybolt' missile on which Britain had relied as an alternative. Hence Britain was forced to accept from the

United States at the Nassau Conference between Mr Macmillian and President Kennedy in December 1962, Polaris missiles with which to arm her nuclear submarines as an effective deterrent, thus exposing the unreality of her claim to be an independent nuclear power. At the same time the United States made the same offer of Polaris missiles to France, but General de Gaulle rejected it.

Moreover, two of the international associations on which Britain had based her 37 post-war foreign policy, the Commonwealth and the 'special relationship' with the United States, were losing their credibility, leaving Europe as a home of last resort. As for the Commonwealth, the new Afro-Asian countries had shown in the Suez crisis in 1956 that their hatred of western imperialism could be stronger than any affection they had for the Commonwealth. In March 1961, when South Africa left the Commonwealth, it was evident that the latter could not, as was hoped, transcend the deep racial divisions within it. As for the United States, Britain had played, as we have seen, a valuable role in tutoring that country in the ways of great-Power politics but it could be argued in 1961, when John F. Kennedy reached the White House, that the United States had by now graduated. Kennedy's meeting with Mr Nikita Khrushchev in Vienna in June 1961 was a foretaste of what was to become familiar: the direct dialogue between America and Russia with no need for an intermediary.

Moreover, did the Russians want to talk with the West in any wider forum? In May 38 1960 Mr Khrushchev journeyed to Paris to meet his American, British and French colleagues at Summit level and then almost immediately returned home, a savage blow to Prime Minister Macmillan, who had worked so hard for the conference. It was the end of the road for four-Power Summit meetings; all that needed to be done there could be more conveniently done at Super-Power level.

The inference that President de Gaulle of France seemed to draw from this was that 39 the wisest course was to try to shut up western Europe into its own fortress, to which France alone held the key. If Britain wanted to exert herself at the Super-Power level, let her, but she must end by becoming a satellite of the United States and hence quite unqualified for EEC membership. The last thing de Gaulle wanted was an EEC controlled by America through her Trojan Horse, Britain. At a press conference in January 1963, without consulting his five partners in the EEC, de Gaulle brutally terminated the negotiations over Britain's candidature for the Communities.

9 The debate in Britain in the 1960s about joining the European Communities was a 40
The second attempt, break with the traditional Right-Left conflict between the parties; there was nothing
1967 especially capitalist or socialist about the EEC, both systems could equally well flourish under its wing. Nevertheless, for a variety of reasons, the Conservative Party was warmer towards the idea of European Union with Britain in it than the Labour Party; the few Liberals in Parliament were at all times pro-European. But both the main parties were divided on grounds which ranged from the emotive to the rational. When Mr Macmillan reversed the direction of British policy on Europe in June 1961 most of his party supported him and the Labour Opposition was cool. When, after toying for two years with the idea of Britain as still having a world role to play, Mr Harold Wilson, who won the general election for Labour in October 1964, decided in spring 1967 to make an application to join the Economic Community under Article 237 of the Rome Treaty, he was supported by the bulk of both parties, the vote in the Commons being a massive 588 in favour. For the moment going into Europe had become a bipartisan policy; the fact that it had, and that Conservative and Labour Prime Ministers alike now backed the European policy, which both in the 1950s had rejected, showed where the logic of events was leading.

Mr Wilson was by no means convinced about Europe when he formed his first 41
government in October 1964; as late as June 1966 he was telling the Parliamentary
Labour Party that Britain could not opt out of her world role (*The Times*, 17 June
1966). But by May 1967 all the signs pointing in the opposite direction were clear;
they were to get clearer as the year progressed. By 1967 Britain had experienced six
more years of economic 'stop-go', culminating in the most severe 'freeze' in July
1966 when Labour's whole policy of economic expansion was forced to a halt. In
November 1967 the Government, after declining to face the inevitable, month after
month, was at length compelled to devalue the pound by 14.3 per cent as a way of
improving the balance of payments.

By 1967, too, there had been six more years' evidence that what Mr Wilson called 42
Britain's 'science-based' industries must have a large market in which to sell their
exports or Britain would slowly die as a great industrial and exporting nation. Meanwhile, the EEC was moving towards a completely free market of well over 200 million
comparatively wealthy people.

In addition, over the six years since 1961 the world political situation had moved 43
on, underlining still further the increasing isolation of Britain in the global balance
of forces. First, the Soviet-American détente had developed: in October 1962
Super-Powers had circumvented the Cuban missile crisis and were beginning to
consolidate their recognition of each other's sphere of influence; in 1963 came the
Partial Nuclear Test Ban treaty which opened the way to further arms control
agreements between two Powers which had now left all other states behind as
far as armaments were concerned; in June 1963 President Kennedy, and again in
October 1966 President Johnson, appealed for steps forward to be made in strengthening the East-West détente. It had become more obvious than ever before that the
United States no longer needed Britain to show her the path to better relations with
the communist world. Britain was needed, if at all, as an ally of the other west
European states in defending their and her interests against possible collusion
between the Super-Powers at Europe's expense.

Secondly, in the mid-1960s the Commonwealth looked increasingly unreal. It was 44
powerless to prevent or bring to an end the Indo-Pakistan war in September 1965
and ultimately the two states came to a temporary understanding at a conference
in Tashkent in January 1966 with Mr Alexei Kosygin, the Soviet Prime Minister,
acting as mediator. More importantly, in November 1965, Mr Ian Smith, the
Prime Minister of Rhodesia, still a colony in British law, illegally declared its independence; there followed months of negotiation for a formula to reconcile Smith's
insistence on continuing white supremacy in Rhodesia and the British demand for
progress towards majority rule, all to no avail. At no point did the British government
contemplate the use of force against Rhodesia; in fact Mr Wilson renounced it at the
outset. This enraged the independent African states in the Commonwealth, already
indignant at Britain's refusal to support mandatory sanctions against the apartheid
regime in South Africa. These Commonwealth reactions did nothing to endear that
institution to the British.

That, in view of these facts, a politician as cool hitherto to European Union as Mr 45
Wilson should have been persuaded to support British membership of the Communities illustrates how conclusive the argument for membership had now become.
But devaluation of the pound, which had for many British people clinched the case
for entry, had placed a powerful argument in the hands of President de Gaulle of
France against *les Anglo-Saxons*. At a press conference in Paris on 27 November 1967
de Gaulle, shifting somewhat his argument from its 1963 position, now declared –
though again without the approval of his five European allies – that Britain was too
weak to stand the strain of entering the Communities and that, if she did enter, she
would be an economic liability to all the others.

The Nassau Conference. President Kennedy (left) offered Polaris missiles to arm British nuclear submarines in place of the cancelled 'Skybolt'. Harold Macmillan accepted the offer much to the annoyance of General de Gaulle.

'Non!' President de Gaulle ends the negotiations for British entry, 1963.

Harold Wilson meets General de Gaulle. The Labour Prime Minister decided to apply for membership in the spring of 1967.

Geoffrey Rippon, Britain's chief negotiator in the successful entry talks.

"Yoo hoo! I'm back."

10

The third attempt, 1970

Mr Wilson had said in May 1967 that if his attempt to join the three Communities – the ECSC, the EEC and Euratom – failed there would be no doubt where the blame lay, always assuming that the terms offered to Britain were 'right', as he later emphasized. The implication was that Britain's application to join was a genuine one and that she was willing to accept all the obligations of membership. This claim appeared even stronger when Mr Edward Heath succeeded Mr Wilson as Prime Minister with a Conservative administration after a general election on 18 June 1970 in which Europe was not an issue. Mr Heath had always been a fervent European: his maiden speech in the House of Commons on 26 June 1950 was a warm welcome to the Schuman Plan and he had led the British team in the negotiations of 1961–3. In 1970 he simply, as he put it, took up the hand in the European negotiations which Mr Wilson had been forced to drop when the 1967 negotiations broke down.

This time the omens were better on the Continental side. General de Gaulle left the French political scene in 1969 and even he seemed to be warming towards British membership of the European Communities before his retirement. His successor, President Georges Pompidou, was less capable of imposing French views on his allies; in any case French fears of *les Anglo-Saxons* had diminished. French bargaining during the endless negotiations which then began and occupied most of 1971 in Brussels – the British side being led by the Chancellor of the Duchy of Lancaster, Mr Geoffrey Rippon – was hard and relentless but the main direction of the discussions was never really in doubt. The final ceremonial signing of the agreements took place in Brussels on 22 January 1972 with a view to Britain – along with Denmark and Ireland[3] – joining the Communities on 1 January 1973.

22 January 1972
Prime Minister Edward Heath signs Britain's accession to the European Communities.
The pile on his right contains those documents and regulations already agreed by the Community

[3]Norway, which was to have joined at the same time, was prevented by a negative note in a popular referendum.

30

After a debate on the terms in the House of Commons in October 1971 Mr Heath 48 obtained his majority for entry but only in the face of Labour opposition, though a group of pro-European Labour MPs, led by Mr Roy Jenkins, disagreed with their leader, Mr Wilson. Mr Wilson disapproved of the Brussels terms on the grounds that the consent of the British people had not been sought, though a popular vote had been held in Denmark, Ireland and Norway, and that the terms were unduly unfavourable to Britain. Though Mr Wilson's position clearly represented an effort to patch up the unity of the Labour Party, which the whole European issue had seriously threatened, the terms were by all accounts tough for any British leader to persuade his people to accept.

"Tell me Mr. Wilson, – Just how long have you been hearing these voices?"

Britain agreed at Brussels that over a transitional period of four and a half years the 49 EEC's Common External Tariff would apply to British industrial exports to third countries, there being free trade in such goods within the enlarged Common Market at the end of the transition period. As to farm goods, the EEC's Common Agricultural Policy (CAP) would be accepted by Britain, this meaning, argued the White Paper, that over the transitional period of six years British retail food prices would rise as a result of accepting the CAP policies by something like 2.5 per cent a year, representing a rise in the cost of living of 0.5 per cent a year. As to the contentious question of the British contribution to the common Community budget, this was calculated according to a complicated mathematical formula, the upshot being that as from 1978 Britain would be paying an estimated £300 million to the expenses of the Communities.

New Zealand, the Commonwealth country perhaps the hardest hit by Britain's new 50 policy since 85 per cent of the export earnings of her butter and cheese industries come from Britain, would have her sales of butter to Britain reduced by 4 per cent a year until 1978, when 80 per cent of her former entitlement would be reached; her cheese exports, however, would be reduced by stages to only 20 per cent of former entitlements by 1977. But New Zealand benefited from the guaranteed price laid down by the Community for butter, which was substantially higher than she was getting only a year or two before.

31

As for the other Commonwealth interests affected by the Brussels Agreement, 51
the Commonwealth Sugar Agreement, which facilitated cane sugar imports from
the Commonwealth into Britain, and which would expire in February 1975, would
be replaced by another agreement between the EEC and Commonwealth sugar
producers. Various forms of association with the European Communities were provided for the independent Commonwealth countries in Africa and the Pacific. The
EEC was to negotiate later with India, Pakistan, Ceylon, Malaysia and Singapore to
replace the favourable arrangements they formerly had with Britain; and Australia
and Canada were to have special arrangements made for them to cover the impact
on them of the Common External Tariff of the EEC (Cmnd 4715, 1971).[4]

The long way forward into Europe for Britain was now ended. The terms of entry, 52
especially the anticipated rise in food prices and their implication for the Commonwealth, were hard, though this was partly because Britain delayed so long in accepting the basic principles of the Communities: had she signed the Rome Treaty in 1957
along with the others, much which in 1971 she had to accept she might have changed.
No one knew whether this momentous step for Britain would turn out successfully,
though some of the doubts in Britain seemed to derive from a feeling of inferiority
complex. Certainly a change of direction for Britain could alter the atmosphere of
lethargy which many foreigners believed Britain had lived in since 1945. Though
many adjustments in British life needed to be made, Europe to the hopeful looked
in January 1973 like a new adventure after the disappointments of the past.

The beginning of the new adventure. The Union Jack is nailed to the mast outside the Community
Headquarters in Brussels

[4]For the Brussels terms in detail see Command Paper 4715 of July 1971, *Britain and the European Communities*,
HMSO.

References

Harrod, Sir R (1963) *The British Economy*, New York and London, McGraw-Hill.

Comments and questions

Having studied this article you should be able to answer the questions below. (Refer back to the text if necessary.) Further comments which draw your attention to points in the text, and give suggestions for further thought are to be found in the Supplementary Material under 'Further comments on Unit 1'.

6 In which particular ways was Britain's position at the end of the Second World War different from that of her Continental neighbours? What were the implications of these for Britain's attitude to European integration?

7 How important in influencing your views at the time of British entry was the emphasis on the 'Common Market' aspect of the EEC? (See paragraph 27 and pages 5 and 82.) How much more than a 'Common Market' is the EEC intended to be?

8 List six or so factors which the author considers important in understanding Britain's decision to join the EEC. Do these factors mean that the argument for membership was conclusive as Northedge maintains? (Paragraph 45.)

9 In 1972 there were various courses of action open to Britain other than joining the EEC. List these and note down some of the points for and against each option. If we had not joined the EEC which option would you have considered preferable?

Further reading

Miriam Camps (1964) *Britain and the European Community, 1955–1963*, London, Oxford University Press.

The standard work on this theme, which also relates British policy to the general development of the Communities. Detailed and perceptive.

Ian Davidson (1971) *Britain and the making of Europe*, London, MacDonald.

A good short account of the period 1965–71.

David Spanier (1972) *Europe, Our Europe*, London, Secker and Warburg.

A good account, by *The Times* correspondent, of the successful negotiations for British entry.

Uwe Kitzinger (1973) *Diplomacy and Persuasion: How Britain joined the Common Market*, London, Thames and Hudson.

A more detailed and analytical account, with especial emphasis on the internal British scene. Contains extensive data on attitudes to entry, and their evolution over time.

Pierre Uri (ed.) (1968) *From Commonwealth to Common Market*, Harmondsworth, Penguin.

Christopher Mayhew *et al.* (1971) *Europe: A Case for Going In*, London, Harrap.

These two books set out the case for entry.

Douglas Evans (ed.) (1971) *Destiny or Delusion: Britain and the Common Market*, London, Gollancz.

William Pickles (1967) *Britain and Europe – How Much has Changed?*, London, Blackwell.

These two argue the case against entry.

Section 3
Introduction, comments and questions on
'Time-lags in Political Psychology' Uwe Kitzinger

Contents

Course team introduction

In 'Time-lags in Political Psychology' Kitzinger advances the idea that in the case of Britain's attitudes towards the EEC there has been a 'time-lag' between membership being in Britain's interest, and recognition of that fact by Government and public resulting in action.

This is another aspect of the interpretation put forward by Northedge, as there are suggestions that once people realized where Britain's best interests lay – i.e. inside the Communities – then membership was but a matter of time and asking.

Kitzinger's thesis raises issues far wider than those relating to the EEC alone. There are many other situations to which his argument applies. It may help you to think of other occasions in recent history, or indeed, at a lower level, in your own personal experience, where you believe Kitzinger's thesis is helpful in understanding what is happening. However, do not allow this to divert you from getting to grips with the argument in relation to the EEC.

As you read the article note down the main features of the argument. This reading is to be found in the Reader on pages 7–22. Turn to it before reading further.

Comments and questions

Having studied the article you should be able to answer the questions below (refer back to the text if necessary). You may also like to take part in the activity suggested.

Further comments which draw your attention to points in the text, and give suggestions for further thought are to be found in the Supplementary Material under 'Further comments on Unit 1'.

10 As with question 8, list six or so factors which this author considers important in understanding Britain's decision to join the EEC. Compare the two lists and note the differences. Accepting that Kitzinger is in basic agreement with Northedge's interpretation of events, explain what his thesis of a 'time-lag in political psychology' adds to the argument.

11 On page 21 of the Reader Kitzinger's article gives the results of the opinion survey you completed for yourself at the beginning of the Unit (pp. 10–11). If you have time, use these same questions to conduct a survey amongst your friends and acquaintances. Compare your results with those given by Kitzinger, and attempt to account for any discrepancies which may emerge. If you wish to make a more comprehensive analysis, you could further break down your results by age, sex and occupation. For example, compare the answers of those aged 16–21 with the answers of those over 21.

Contents

Roy Pryce Director in Information Directorate-General of the Commission of the European Communities, since April 1973. Previously Professorial Fellow and founding Director (1965–73) of the Centre for Contemporary European Studies of the University of Sussex, during which time he directed a research programme and taught about the European Communities. He was also a visiting professor at the College of Europe, Bruges. Publications include *Europe after de Gaulle* (1969 Penguin) (joint author, with J. Pinder) and *The Political Future of the European Community* (1962, Marshbank). This paper is adapted from Chapter 1 of *The Politics of the European Community* (1973, Butterworths).

Course team introduction

Discussion of motivation recurs throughout much of the reading material. Some motives remain constant over a long period: for example the hope of economic growth through co-operation; whereas others disappear or new ones emerge. An example of changing motives is in Kitzinger's paper when he writes: 'World federalism in general, and the specific European problem of Germany, thus formed the first two mainsprings of West European integration' (Reader p. 12). Is world federation a mainspring today? Obviously, no. And if it can still be argued that a 'German problem' exists, it is very different from that of the late 1940s and early 1950s. Turning to more recent motives, the 1972 Paris Summit Communiqué (p. 78) gives a very clear indication of those identified by Europe's political leaders of today.

Motives vary not only over time but among people at the same time. The most obvious example in this unit is the difference in motivation between the British and the original members of the EEC; but differences are not confined to those between nations. As 'The Great Debate' (Reader, pp. 29–42) reveals there have been and continue to be substantial differences within Britain.

Pryce's paper summarizes the history of Europe in the years since the end of the Second World War, concentrating in particular on the steps towards the foundation of the European Communities and charting their growth and expansion since 1958. It will help you to identify the major European institutions and to understand their historical relationship to one another. Their structural relationship will be dealt with in Unit 2.

As you read through the article try to identify three strands of information:

a   Note the motives behind the movement towards European unity.

b   Note the name of the major institutions referred to, and the initials by which they are known. This will help you throughout the course. You can also refer to the 'Glossary of Western European Organizations' for this (pp. 74–6).

c   Endeavour to get clear in your mind the broad chronological sequence of events. You do not have to learn off a list of dates, unless you like learning lists of dates!

(Reference to the 'Chronology of events in the formation of the European Communities' will help you in these two latter tasks, and you may find it useful to add to it key dates of your own as reference points in the time scale. For example, many people remember the Cuban Crisis of October 1962 as a significant event, or Suez in 1956, or Auntie Lily's wedding!)

The Historical Development of the European Communities
Roy Pryce

1
Introduction   The origin of the desire for European unity can be traced far back in European   1
history. For many centuries, however, it was no more than a dream. The vision of a peaceful and united Europe was sustained by a handful of far-sighted individuals such as Erasmus, Emmanuel Kant and Jeremy Bentham in the face of the assertion of the nation state as the dominant form of political organization, a trend which reached its peak in the second half of the nineteenth century. Their pleas were, however, isolated protests: they were overwhelmed by the clamour of nationalist movements and the persistent conflicts between the major European states as they sought to assert their power and extend their frontiers.

It was only after the second of two world wars, both of which originated in Europe – 2
and which left a large part of the continent devastated – that effective steps were
taken to give substance to the old dream. Ironically, Europeans were then confronted
by a continent which was in some ways more divided than ever before as a result of the
tensions that had developed between the victorious Allies. The positions reached by
the Soviet Army on the one hand, and that of the western Allies on the other, had
become by 1948 an iron curtain, on each side of which rival groups, each fearful of
the other, had been constructed.

At the same time European countries found themselves overshadowed by the power 3
of their rival protectors, the United States and the Soviet Union, and dependent
on them for their security. In the east this dependence was all the greater because of
the political needs of the new regimes established by the communist parties. There,
as long as Stalin remained in power, party leaders looked nervously to Moscow for
support. Although subsequent Soviet leaders have on the whole exercised their
political tutelage by less draconian methods, the overwhelming economic and
political power of the USSR with regard to the smaller socialist states of eastern
Europe has been such as to determine both the form and content of the various
forms of political, military and economic co-operation which have developed between
this group of countries. The main formal organizations set up for this purpose are
the Council for Mutual Economic Co-operation (COMECON) and the Warsaw
Pact (Ransom, 1973).

In western Europe, on the other hand, the influence exerted by the United States – 4
though strong and pervasive in the early post-war years – has not been as critical
a factor in determining the steps taken towards closer unity by those countries lying
within its own sphere of influence. Increasingly, it has been the west European countries themselves who have dictated the pace and content of their own moves
towards greater unity, the central role in which has now been assumed by the nine-
member European Community, which Britain (together with Denmark and
Ireland) joined in January 1973.

The development of the Community has, however, been a slow and difficult process. 5
It was by no means certain when the first steps towards economic and political
integration were taken by six continental states in 1950 that their ambitions would
be realized. And subsequently the continuing strength of the nation state has been
amply demonstrated. The process of economic and political integration inaugurated
by the Six has certainly brought major changes both in the relations between its
members and also in the relations between western Europe and the rest of the world.
But even after more than twenty years western Europe is still far from its ultimate
goal of effective unity.

As the following account will show, the process of integration has been far from 6
smooth: and progress has always been dependent on ways being found of reconciling
national interests which have rarely, if ever, been identical. A critical role at each
stage has been exercised by national leaders, and particularly by those of the larger
countries. The ability or otherwise of such leaders to agree has been of crucial
importance: and for the foreseeable future this will remain the case, as our part of the
world seeks to extend the range of policy areas where its nations agree to take
decisions together, rather than individually.

2 The formal initiative which led to the creation of the first European Community 7
From the Schuman was taken by the French Foreign Minister, M. Robert Schuman, on 9 May 1950.
Plan to the Treaty of He then proposed, that French and German production of coal and steel should be
Paris (1950–1) placed under a common High Authority 'within the framework of an organization

NATO MEMBERS ▦
and Canada, USA, Iceland
France withdrew from NATO in 1966
WARSAW PACT MEMBERS ▦

open to the participation of the other countries of Europe'. But this, he explained, was only the first step towards a much more far-reaching objective (Pryce, 1962):

In this way there will be realized, simply and speedily, that fusion of interests which is indispensable to the establishment of an economic community; and that will be the leaven from which may grow a wider and deeper community between countries long opposed to one another by bloody conflicts. . . . This proposal will build the first concrete foundation of a European federation which is indispensable to the preservation of peace.

Five other countries – Belgium, the Netherlands, Italy, Luxembourg and West Germany – responded favourably to the proposal, and in April 1951 a treaty was signed in Paris creating the European Coal and Steel Community. This was established, with its headquarters in Luxembourg, in the summer of 1952. 8

The creation of the six-nation Community marked an important new development in the post-war history of Europe. It took place against a background of a series of initiatives which had been taken in the closing years of the Second World War, and in its immediate aftermath, which had sought to encourage closer co-operation between various groups of countries in western Europe. One of the earliest of these 9 was the conclusion in London in 1944 of an agreement by the three exiled governments of Belgium, the Netherlands and Luxembourg to set up a customs union within the framework of a common organization known as BENELUX. The Scandinavian countries, for their part, also soon resumed their own search for closer co-operation – mainly in the fields of social and legal affairs – which had been interrupted by the war. This led, in 1952, to the establishment of the Nordic Council, in which parliamentarians joined with governments to promote closer unity.

Parallel with these efforts strong pressures also developed to provide a framework 10 on a wider basis through which the democratic countries of western Europe could work more closely together. In part these pressures were related to the Cold War situation, and the need for the countries of western Europe to rely on the United States for their defence. It was this need which led, in 1948, to the creation of the Brussels Treaty Organization – a body grouping Britain, France and the Benelux countries which provided for co-operation in military, political and social matters; and in the following year to the signature of the North Atlantic Treaty in which the United States pledged itself to the defence of western Europe.

The needs of economic reconstruction also led to close US involvement in the affairs 11 of western Europe: the generous offer of Marshall Aid in 1947 being made on condition that the countries which accepted such aid should themselves agree on how it should be handled between them. The response of the west European countries, led by Britain and France, led in 1948 to the creation by sixteen countries of a permanent body to foster economic co-operation: the Organization for European Economic Co-operation (OEEC).[1]

At the same time various groups of Europeans themselves were also urging the need 12 for closer political co-operation.

These pressures were by no means wholly related to the Cold War situation. In part 13 they drew their inspiration from the vision of a united Europe which had long been nurtured in the continent, both by visionaries and men of action. More immediately they drew on the determination of many of those who had taken part in the resistance movements during the war to seek a new framework in which European countries could at last live peacefully together. And to these was added the powerful voice of Winston Churchill who urged the need for reconciliation between former enemies, and the creation – as he put it in his Zurich speech of September 1946 – of 'a kind of United States of Europe'. It was as a result of a confluence of these various pressures that in 1949 thirteen countries set up the Council of Europe consisting of a Consultative Assembly (composed of parliamentarians) and a Committee of Ministers (representing national governments) with the general purpose of promoting closer unity between them (PEP, 1968).

These achievements masked, however, significant differences of purpose between 14 the countries of western Europe. These had been dramatically expressed at the Congress of Europe held at The Hague in May 1948. This meeting, which brought together some 800 distinguished protagonists of closer unity, had great difficulty in reconciling the demands of some of those from the continental countries for radical measures designed to reduce the role of the nation state with British and Scandinavian attitudes which, while favouring closer unity, wished to see it achieved on the basis of co-operation between national governments.

As far as the British were concerned there were two main reasons for the position 15 they adopted. The first was that their own wartime experience had strengthened rather than weakened their sense of national pride and achievement. The second

[1] In 1960 the tasks of the OEEC were reshaped and its membership enlarged to include Japan. At the same time its name changed to the Organization for Economic Co-operation and Development (OECD).

was that they saw themselves as not only a European but also a world power. The Churchillian concept of British influence resting on three overlapping circles of relationships – with the United States, the Commonwealth, and Europe – neatly summed up what the overwhelming majority of the British political elite instinctively felt. We were with Europe, but not of it. It followed that a condition for British participation in moves towards closer unity in Europe should not constrain her freedom of action in other directions.

The Château de la Muette, headquarters of the OECD, Organization for Economic Co-operation and Development

Winston Churchill. In September 1946 he called for 'a kind of United States of Europe'

The Headquarters of the Council of Europe, Strasbourg

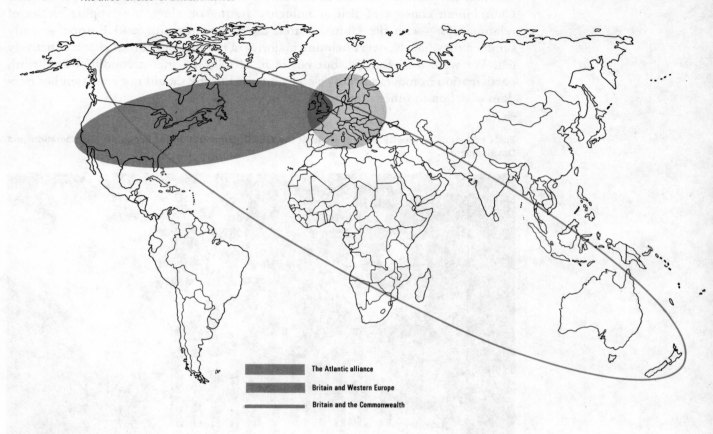

The Atlantic alliance

Britain and Western Europe

Britain and the Commonwealth

It was this view which lay at the heart of the policy vigorously pursued in the 16 immediate post-war years by the Labour government, and which largely conditioned the content and shape of the European organizations which were created. Britain was then in a position to call the tune.

3
The Coal and Steel
Community

The French initiative of 1950 in proposing a Coal and Steel Community was the first 17 major challenge to the British position. For if the forms of intergovernmental co-operation which had been developed up to that point suited the United Kingdom very well, they were distinctly less satisfactory for France. That country was above all concerned about relations with her eastern neighbour, Germany, at whose hands she had suffered defeat, or near defeat, on three successive occasions in the recent past. Although Germany was now divided, and West Germany had not yet regained the status of an independent state (though the Federal Republic had been recognized by the West in 1949), French leaders were nevertheless concerned by the rapid economic recovery which had taken place and the change in US policy which now saw a revived West Germany not as a pastoral no-man's-land, but as a potential bulwark against the Soviet Union. In this situation there was a risk, from the French point of view, of yet again being confronted by a very powerful neighbour on her eastern frontier. There was matter enough for dispute between the two, not least the uncertain future fate of the Ruhr and the Saar whose mineral resources and heavy industries were a major concern to both countries. As relations between them began to deteriorate, fears also began to revive (and not only in France) that history might again be repeated unless action was taken.

44

Traditionally France had sought to deal with the German problem by alliance with 18
Britain. This policy had not, however, prevented France being invaded. Although
in 1947 the Treaty of Dunkirk was concluded with Britain which pledged her support
against the danger of a revival of a military threat from Germany, the general British
stance towards Europe gave little grounds for French confidence in her ally. Some
greater guarantee was therefore needed. The answer eventually arrived at was the
novel and radical solution of embracing her historical enemy.

This step required both courage and imagination. The imagination was largely 19
supplied by Jean Monnet, then head of the French national planning authority.

He had had a long experience of co-operative international ventures, and had 20
reached the conclusion that a bold step forward was the only way of providing an
effective new framework for common action in western Europe. It was he who already
in 1940 had proposed a Franco-British political union: together with a number of
his associates, he now worked out an equally bold plan. The idea of some type of
international control over those heavy industries which alone could provide the
sinews of war was not in itself new: but what was new in the scheme which Monnet
drew up was the coupling of this idea with the notion of an eventual United States of
Europe. It was this plan – still little more than the germ of an idea – which Monnet
succeeded in selling to Schuman, and he in turn to the French cabinet. Before anyone could change their minds, and before the full implications had been realized by
more than a handful of people, Schuman announced the new initiative to a crowded
press conference.

Jean Monnet. It was his 'germ of an idea' which   Robert Schuman, who gave his name to the Plan
grew into the Coal and Steel Community   which led to the Coal and Steel Community

The tactic of surprise paid off handsomely, but it still required courage and deter- 21
mination to translate the Schuman Plan into reality (Diebold, 1959). One big hazard
was the British refusal to take part in the negotiations: a decision which was reached
after an intensive and rather agonized exchange of messages across the Channel in
the weeks immediately following Schuman's announcement. On the British side
there was a good deal of irritation at being confronted by what was considered to be
a *fait accompli*, and resistance to the French concern that there should be a prior
commitment to the type of organization they proposed. The Labour government,
having recently nationalized the coal industry in Britain, and being committed (if

somewhat more hesitantly) to the similar treatment of the steel industry, was understandably opposed to the transfer of authority to some rather ill-defined body over which it would not have direct control. By this time too, the configuration of political forces which had emerged on the continent, had made it clear that there was no immediate prospect of socialist parties gaining power in the countries of the proposed Community. The idea of a socialist United States of Europe – which had originally been espoused by some leading figures on the left-wing of the British Labour Party – was now regarded as a chimera. But in addition to all these objections, there was fundamentally little sympathy with the idea of any deep British commitment to continental western Europe, and both opposition to – and little belief in the practicability of – a federal union which was mentioned in the Schuman Plan as its ultimate objective.

The British refusal to join in negotiations did not, however, prevent other countries 22 going ahead on the basis of the French plan. There was little expectation in Britain at the time that they would get very far, and few who realized how significant a turning point had been reached. The main factor in the situation was the willingness of the Federal Republic to respond to the French initiative. This was due primarily to Konrad Adenauer, who shared with Schuman (a fellow Catholic) a conviction of the necessity of overcoming traditional Franco-German rivalry. He was also intent on binding the new German nation into the west, fearing the consequences of a policy of flirtation with the Soviet Union both for his own country and Europe as a whole. In Italy the Austrian-born premier Alcide de Gasperi was equally anxious to find a framework in which Italy could resume its position among the nations of western Europe, and one which would offer a stable economic background in which the country could deal with its own internal problems.

Konrad Adenauer,
Chancellor of the Federal Republic of Germany.
He was convinced of the necessity of
overcoming traditional Franco-German rivalry

Alcide de Gasperi.
As Premier, he sought a framework within which
Italy could resume its position among the
nations of western Europe

The trio of Benelux countries, for their part, were already committed to a customs 23 union and looking beyond this to a closer economic union. Once their larger neighbours moved in the same direction, they could not afford to stay outside: in any case there were many among their leaders who were determined supporters of closer European unity (Haas, 1968).

In a remarkably short period of time – less than a year – these six were able to agree 24
on a treaty setting up a European Coal and Steel Community. Their basic decision
was to establish a common market for coal and steel, to establish a series of rules
for the conduct and regulation of the common market, and to create a set of
institutions to supervise its development. Relatively few serious problems were
encountered in the course of the negotiations, though those countries which feared
the impact of freer competition on either the coal or steel sector pressed for special
measures which would allow them to alleviate any resulting problems. Such
measures were in fact provided for the Belgian coal industry and Italian steel.

One important issue which proved somewhat more difficult was the extent of the 25
powers of the High Authority proposed by the French. This was conceived of as an
independent body which would regulate the common market in the interests of all
its members free from direction from individual member governments. Although
the French had made agreement to the principle of such a 'supranational' body as
a pre-condition for participation in negotiations, it emerged from the negotiations
in a somewhat modified form. All the other countries were understandably hesitant
to give such a body *carte blanche*. What they did therefore was to construct a
treaty which laid down in very considerable detail the rules which were to govern
the operation of the common market for coal and steel. There was clearly much less
risk in a supranational body administering such rules, than in allowing it to establish
the rules itself. Under pressure from the Netherlands in particular a body representing the national governments was also created: a Council of Ministers to which
the High Authority had to refer various types of proposed decisions, and whose other
main task was to see that the actions of the High Authority did not conflict with other
areas of national economic policy. A Court of Justice was also provided, to which
governments, firms and individuals, as well as the High Authority itself, could appeal.
And in an attempt to ensure that the High Authority was responsible to someone,
a Parliamentary Assembly was to be set up, to which the High Authority would
report annually, and by whom it could be dismissed.

Under the energetic leadership of Jean Monnet, who was appointed President of the 26
first nine-man High Authority, the task of implementing the treaty began in August
1952, shortly after it had been approved by the six national parliaments. Luxembourg
had reluctantly agreed to provide the site for the institutions of the new Community,[2]
and it was from there that first decisions of the High Authority began to flow in the
autumn of that year. The common market for coal was opened in February 1953;
that for steel a little later, in May. Arrangements were also put in hand for price
publicity, a start was made on implementing the agreed rules of competition, and
the other provisions of the treaty. Somewhat to the surprise of the men in Luxembourg, the decisions were accepted, even if it was not long before issues arose in
which the High Authority found itself in conflict both with individual member
governments and firms.

The early years of the new Community were nevertheless relatively smooth. This 27
was a period when economic growth was proceeding apace; the problems that arose
were mainly technical in nature; and the fears that had been expressed in some
quarters during the negotiations of wholesale unemployment or bankruptcies
proved quite unfounded.

It was not in fact until 1958 that the Community found itself confronted by a major 28
crisis: stocks of unsold coal began to accumulate as the industry found itself unable
to compete with imports of cheaper American coal and the increasing use of oil.
The High Authority sought the agreements of the member governments to the

[2]At this stage Luxembourg had not realized the advantages of being the headquarters of an international
organization: its national motto was 'We wish to remain as we are'.

declaration of a state of 'manifest crisis' which under the treaty would have allowed it to fix production quotas and take other measures to deal with the situation. In May 1959, however, the Council of Ministers refused its agreement, and although subsequently it allowed the High Authority to take a series of piecemeal measures (including the temporary isolation of the Belgian coal market), national governments increasingly began to take unilateral action to safeguard the interests of their domestic industries. This development coincided both with a marked decline in the political leadership of the High Authority itself and the creation of two new Communities. Several of the senior officials who, with Monnet, had played a major part in establishing the Community now moved to Brussels, and it was there that the political spotlight was now focused. The Community continued to exist, but in a minor key. In July 1967 its executive was merged with that of the other two Communities: although juridically the ECSC remains a separate entity it has ceased to have a clear positive identity of its own. Its most important work was accomplished early in its history when it succeeded quite remarkably in the task set for it by those who conceived it: a pilot project and first step along the road towards eventual economic and political union.

4
Two abortive
projects: the
European Defence
Community and the
European Political
Community (1952–4)

Although two new Communities were created alongside the ECSC in less than 29 eight years after the first announcement of the Schuman Plan, this was only after the Six had suffered a severe setback in the intervening period. This was due to the failure of a project for a Defence Community, for which a treaty was signed in May 1952, and with which was associated a complementary proposal for a Political Community.

The proposal for a Defence Community was again made by the French, and – like the 30 Schuman Plan – was largely inspired by Monnet. But unlike the Schuman Plan its content and timing was not determined by Monnet or the French Government so much as by external pressures. The initiative was the result of the outbreak of the Korean War in June 1950 and American fears that this might bring in its train a Soviet move against western Europe. They therefore decided that it was now a matter of urgency that the Federal Republic should make a military contribution to NATO. Monnet's reaction was to see in this proposal both a threat and an opportunity: a threat because German contingents in NATO might lead in the direction of a new German army and the creation of a new roadblock on the way towards a political union; an opportunity because the proposal could perhaps be diverted to increaes the scope of integration by extending it to defence and military matters.

He therefore proposed that a limited rearmament of West Germany should take 31 place within the framework of a European army under the aegis of a European Defence Community modelled on the proposed Coal and Steel Community (negotiations for which were then under way under his chairmanship). With some difficulty he succeeded in selling the idea to the French government, whose Prime Minister, René Pleven, presented it to the French National Assembly in October 1950. This plan – the 'Pleven Plan' – was approved in outline at that stage by 343 votes to 225.

Once again the British were invited to take part in negotiations, but refused to do 32 so: and although there was a change of government in Britain in 1951 while the negotiations were still proceeding the incoming Conservative administration also decided not to take part, although profering external support for it. This was a severe blow to the protagonists of the EDC, who had been encouraged by earlier Churchillian support for a European army to believe that a Conservative government would join. Within the Six themselves opinion was much more divided on the proposal than it had been on the Schuman Plan, and a particularly bitter conflict developed in France itself. There was strong opposition both to the rearmament of

West Germany and to placing French military forces under European control. The Communists and Gaullists (then a rising political force) both opposed the project, as did also a substantial body of opinion in the Socialist Party.

Together they made a formidable body of dissent. The negotiators themselves had considerable difficulty in resolving the complex political and technical problems which the proposal presented, though they succeeded in reaching agreement on a treaty for the new Community in Paris in May 1952. 33

Before it could come into effect however, it required ratification by the six national parliaments. In each of them there were heated and lengthy debates: after almost two years only four of them had ratified it. In the meantime the Korean War had come to an end and Stalin had died: the immediate pressures that had given rise to the proposal had ceased to operate. Italy and France still hesitated to press ratification of the treaty to a vote. In both, the ruling governmental coalitions were highly unstable and fearful of provoking defeat by bringing the matter to a vote. Eventually Pierre Mendès-France in France decided to put the matter to the test, after an abortive attempt to alter the treaty in an attempt to gain more support for it. The critical vote took place in the National Assembly in Paris on 30 August 1954: on a procedural issue it was rejected by a vote of 319 to 264, with 43 abstentions (Lerner and Aron, 1957). 34

This vote spelled the end of the project, and with it a parallel and related proposal for a European Political Community. The need for an effective political authority at the Community level had become apparent during the EDC negotiations: Article 43 of the EDC treaty provided that an assembly of parliamentarians should work out proposals for submission to the ministers. On the initiative of Schuman and de Gasperi action was taken in September 1952 on this proposal in advance of ratification, and an enlarged version of the Coal and Steel Community's Assembly (which had by that time just come into being) was charged with drawing up proposals by March 1953. This they duly did, in a document which proposed a bicameral Parliament (consisting of a directly-elected Peoples' Chamber, and an indirectly-elected Senate); a European Executive Council, whose president was to be elected by the Senate, and which would be collectively responsible to (and dismissible by) the Parliament; a Council of Ministers and a Court of Justice. The proposal, however, was never seriously considered by the ministers, and after the failure of the EDC it was consigned to the archives. One of the pillars on which this ambitious edifice was to have been built had collapsed. All that now remained was the Coal and Steel Community. 35

5 Relance: from Messina to Rome (1955–7)

This failure was a bitter blow to those who had staked their hopes on the six-nation Community: it called into question the whole strategy which Monnet had conceived of advancing from one sector to another in pursuit of eventual economic and political union. The viability of the Six as a group was also at stake, for in the aftermath of the EDC it was the British who reasserted themselves and succeeded swiftly in picking up the pieces. They proposed that a German military contribution to NATO should be organized within the framework of an expanded Brussels Treaty Organization, a body originally set up in 1948 by Britain, France and the Benelux countries for their military defence and the promotion of political and cultural co-operation. This proposal, though it contained provisions for majority voting on certain issues, effectively left control of military forces in the hands of each national government: it therefore avoided the most controversial feature of the now-defunct EDC. At the same time, however, it contained provisions restricting the Germans to twelve divisions, banning the production on West German soil of 36 atomic, biological and chemical weapons, and instituting an inspection system. It therefore contained safeguards against an uncontrolled German military expansion. These proposals speedily found acceptance on the part of the governments of the Six,[3] and a treaty was signed in Paris in October 1954 setting up the new organization: Western European Union (PEP, 1968). There were some who hoped that WEU might provide a springboard from which Britain and the Six might together go forward. This, however, was not the British intention. The initiative remained across the Channel, and again it was Jean Monnet who played a considerable part in relaunching the Six along the road towards a further instalment of integration. The strength of the political will to undertake this can be judged by the speed with which recovery from the deep depression and disappointment of the frustrating fight for EDC was achieved.

Very rapidly there was a proliferation of plans for a *relance*. There was general agree- 37 ment that the way forward lay through extending the experience of ECSC in the realm of economic integration. There was considerable disagreement, however, on how this could best be attempted. Monnet himself was strongly in favour of another venture in sector integration, and his own preference went to nuclear power. Here was a realm apparently free from entrenched national interests: it promised to be an expanding and forward-looking area of technology, and one in which the high cost of research and development would make closer co-operation highly desirable if not essential. At the same time Monnet hoped that joint action could be accompanied by a common decision to foreswear the production of nuclear weapons: in other words, integration could be released from the unfortunate connection it had acquired with weapons of war during the period of the EDC, and once again become identified (as it had been in the Schuman Plan) with images of peace.

This idea, however, met with a less than enthusiastic response in the other five. 38 Both the Federal Republic and the Benelux countries, for their part, were much more interested in a general common market than a purely nuclear agency. They were willing to accept the latter, however, as long as it was accompanied by more general economic integration. It was on this basis that they were prepared to go forward, and it was this compromise which provided the essential basis for the formal steps which were now taken to explore the possibilities of a new move forward.

In June 1955 the Foreign Ministers of the Six met in Messina and there agreed to 39 set up an intergovernmental committee to study ways in which 'a fresh advance towards the building of Europe' could be achieved. The meeting itself reached no decision on the various differing strategies which had been suggested, but the nomination shortly afterwards of the Belgian Foreign Minister, Paul-Henri Spaak, to head the committee meant that a powerful new impulse was given to the Messina resolution.

Once again the British were invited to take part, and an official of the Board of 40 Trade was this time despatched to the outskirts of Brussels where in the Chateau de Val Duchesse the Spaak Committee worked intensively on the problem it had been given. One of its critical decisions was that the next stage in economic integration should take the form of a customs union rather than a free trade area: in other words the aim should be not only the removal of internal customs duties, but the erection of a common tariff round the enlarged market, and the development within it of a range of common policies. The arguments put forward in favour of this course were both economic and political – but they were not of a sort to appeal to the British government. It was certainly in favour of easier access to continental markets, but the price at that time appeared too high. One of the most serious objections was that a common tariff would run counter to trading arrangements

[3]Italy was also included as a partner in the new organization.

Paul-Henri Spaak, Foreign Minister of Belgium. He headed the Committee which drew up the Treaties of Rome

with the Commonwealth – and the British did not stay to see whether some compromise arrangement might have been possible – unlike the French who had a not dissimilar problem with regard to their overseas possessions, and who succeeded handsomely at a later stage in persuading their partners to accept a very favourable set of arrangements.

So it was left for the Six to labour on. The Spaak Report, which was presented to the Ministers in April 1956 came out in favour of a compromise solution between those who sought further instalments of sector integration and those who favoured a general common market. It suggested that action should be taken on both fronts, singling out the peaceful uses of nuclear energy as a priority area for sector integration. The Ministers acted rapidly. Meeting in Venice at the end of May they adopted the report as a basis for formal negotiations, and charged the Spaak Committee with the task of drawing up the necessary draft treaties. 41

The major problem during the subsequent negotiations was to devise a package that would not run the risk of a second rejection by the French Assembly. The French negotiators found themselves therefore in a strong diplomatic position. Fearing that French industry, which had traditionally sheltered behind high protective barriers, might find itself in difficulties in a common market, they sought – and were largely successful in obtaining – a series of provisions designed to safeguard their position. At the same time they insisted (against German wishes) that the new Community should adopt a common agricultural policy. The commitment was not spelled out in any detail, but it was to prove a sufficient basis for the French subsequently to exploit in the interests of their farmers. 42

The successful outcome of the negotiations rested essentially on a bargain struck between the French and the Germans, the latter being willing to make a series of concessions to the French, including – at a late stage – the conclusion of a special association agreement for their overseas possessions (mainly in West Africa) in return for the prospect of a greatly expanded tariff-free market for their industrial goods. A complex series of other bargains and side payments was also struck to accommodate the interests of the other members. In many cases these were only achieved with considerable difficulty, and many informed observers in Britain were very dubious whether the treaties would be concluded and ratified (Camps, 1964). 43

51

27 March 1957 Home and dry. While it rained outside the Foreign Ministers of the Six signed the Rome Treaties

But this time, there was no hitch. In a ceremony in Rome on 27 March 1957 – while 44 the rain poured down outside – the six Foreign Ministers signed treaties establishing two new Communities, the European Economic Community (EEC) and the European Atomic Energy Community (Euratom). Ratification was speedily achieved, and the new institutions were able to set to work in Brussels on 1 January 1958.

6
The new
Communities in
action (1958–62)

Contrary to many expectations it was the Economic Community rather than 45 Euratom that led the way in the new phase of integration, and which in its first four years of existence astonished almost everyone by the rapidity with which it made progress in carrying out the tasks allotted to it.

Unlike the treaty setting up the ECSC, the Common Market Treaty was for the most 46 part a framework for action rather than a detailed set of rules. The one major exception to this were the provisions it laid down for the achievement of a customs union. Customs duties between members were to be gradually abolished over a twelve to fifteen year transition period divided into three stages. At the same time, differences between national tariffs towards the outside world were gradually to be aligned to produce a Common External Tariff. The other provisions relating to the free movement of workers and capital, the right of establishment, and the creation of common or harmonized policies in certain crucial areas – such as agriculture, transport, external trade and competition – were much more imprecise. For the most part the Treaty confined itself to general statements of objectives, and indications of the instruments that were to be used to achieve the desired goals. This lack of precision was in part due to the fact of the very wide range of problems which had to be tackled: the negotiators had not had time, nor had they been in a position, to examine many of them in detail. But imprecision was also due to disagreements on many issues between the partners: this was particularly the case with regard to the thorny problem of agriculture.

A great deal therefore depended on the institutions of the new Community, and in 47 particular on the ability of its nine-man Commission to find ways of reconciling these divergent interests. In both of the new Communities the name Commission had been preferred to High Authority: but the change was not simply one of nomenclature. Enthusiasm for 'supranationality' had waned; it had not been possible to agree on the detailed rules for the operation of the Community; and the national governments were anxious to keep as much power as possible in their own hands, at least in the early stages of the development of the general common market. The main task given to the EEC Commission therefore was that of making proposals: decisions were to be taken by the Council of Ministers. The right – virtually an exclusive right – to initiate policy proposals was nevertheless a very important function, and under its first president, Walter Hallstein, the new Commission speedily made its impact.

'I am willing to take up the reins of power again'!
General de Gaulle declares his readiness to return to office as President during the Algerian crisis 1958

Walter Hallstein. First President of the European Commission

It was helped in its task by a number of favourable factors. One of these was the **48** continuing rapid pace of economic growth in the member countries: industrial producers were for the most part in an expansionist frame of mind, and they responded positively to the prospect of the Common Market, and were soon to urge a more rapid rate of tariff dismantlement than had originally been envisaged. There were also a number of favourable political factors. Externally the United States continued to give its support to the Communities: this was particularly important in preventing the British from attempting to intervene to trouble its early development. The British Government after its withdrawal from the Spaak Committee, was certainly not pleased to see the Six succeed in setting up the new Communities. It undertook a major reappraisal of their policy and having decided against any direct attempt to wreck the Communities – came up with the idea of a wider free trade area of which both Britain, the Community and other OEEC countries could be part. The British argued that it would be in everyone's interest to extend the area of free trade in industrial goods and that this indeed had been one of the early objectives of the OEEC.[4] From the British point of view it was a splendid idea: it reconciled a continuation of preferential arrangements with the Commonwealth with open access to European markets; avoided the difficult problem of agriculture (which was initially omitted altogether from the scheme); and politically offered at least the possibility of containing the development of the Communities.

There was initially sufficient support from the free-trade minded members of the **49** Six – notably the Germans and the Dutch – to make it appear a viable project. Agreement was reached in the OEEC to undertake negotiations, which eventually got under way in 1958 under the chairmanship of Reginald Maudling. There was

[4]The British did not dwell on the fact that at that stage they had opposed the idea.

little in the scheme, however, to appeal to the French. To them all it offered was increased competition in their industrial markets: hardly a welcome prospect. Nevertheless, for some time they were uncertain of the policy which they should follow.

In May 1958 the Fourth Republic was plunged into its final crisis over Algeria, a 50 crisis which was resolved by the return to power of de Gaulle. At this point prospects seemed distinctly gloomy for the new Community. Disagreements between its members over the British proposal were reflected even in the Commission – and now it was faced by a French Head of State who had consistently and vehemently opposed the creation of the Communities. De Gaulle, however, decided to throw his weight against the Free Trade Area proposal. In retrospect it is not difficult to see why. From his point of view it offered a series of economic disadvantages and no counter-vailing political gains. It could well lead the British and their friends to a position from which they could dictate the future economic and political development of western Europe. And although de Gaulle admired the British he had no reason – particularly in the light of his wartime experiences – to play a subordinate role to them once again. The French put forward a series of counter proposals and rallied (with the aid of the Commission) the support of their partners in the Community. In November 1958 the negotiations broke down. Subsequently the British, under pressure from the Scandinavian countries, decided to go ahead with the construction of a smaller industrial free trade area. This led in 1960 to the setting up of the European Free Trade Association (EFTA) with seven members – Britain, Denmark, Norway, Sweden, Switzerland, Portugal and Ireland – with its headquarters in Geneva. Its aim was both to demonstrate that a free trade area could work and, hopefully, to exert pressure on the Community to arrive at an agreement with its members (Camps, 1964).

Its immediate effect, however, was to remove British pressure on the Community. 51 This, coupled with the decision of de Gaulle to maintain French obligations under the Rome treaties and the measures he took at the end of 1958 to strengthen the French economy, paved the way for the early success of the EEC.

The first set of internal tariff cuts – a modest 10 per cent – were duly carried out on 52 1 January 1959, and by the end of the following year the Council of Ministers agreed to a first move towards a common agricultural policy. In devising a strategy to develop such a policy the Commission, and in particular its Member with a special responsibility for agriculture, the Dutchman Sicco Mansholt, played a critical part. It was he who decided that priority should be given to the organization of markets and the establishment of common prices; who devised the mechanism by which these were to be achieved; and who steered the Commission's proposals through the Council of Ministers.

In this process a series of bargains was struck between the member states, sometimes 53 within the agricultural sector itself, sometimes between that sector and other policy areas. Such bargains involved the careful construction and negotiation of elaborate 'packages' which from time to time became the object of marathon sessions of the Council of Ministers. One such notable package was the outcome of a series of ministerial meetings which went on almost without interruption from 4 December 1961 until the early hours of 14 January 1962. This feat of endurance involved forty-five separate meetings (seven of them at night), 137 hours of discussion, with 214 hours in sub-committee: 582,000 pages of documents – and three heart attacks (Lindberg, 1963). Out of it came a series of agreements detailing the first substantial

The Headquarters of the European Free Trade Association in Geneva. The aim of EFTA 'was both to demonstrate that a free trade area could work and hopefully, to exert pressure on the Community to arrive at an agreement with its members'

measures laying the foundations of the common marketing arrangements for agriculture, an agreement on how the early stages of the Common Market agricultural policy were to be financed, and on the regulation of competition between firms in the Community. As a result the Six agreed to move to the second stage of the EEC's transitional period.

With the speeding up of the timetable for tariff reductions on industrial goods 54 (agreed during 1960) and considerable progress towards a common policy for agriculture the EEC began to assume an air of success. This was increased by an initiative taken by de Gaulle late in 1959 which led to negotiations designed to lead to a treaty of political union – that is, the extension of the scope of integration to matters of defence, foreign policy and culture. The French leader had now come round to the view that the Community of the Six was not only a useful economic grouping but one which could serve French political interests. He instinctively believed that French leadership (certainly as long as it remained in his hands) would predominate: he was confident that he could deal with the Germans, and he had a low opinion of the other members of the Community. The proposals for negotiations on political union were nevertheless welcomed by the other governments: it accorded with the aims to which they had agreed in the preamble to the treaties of Rome – 'an ever closer union among the European peoples' – and the other five no doubt considered that they could contain any French ambitions to dictate policy within such a union, though from the beginning the Dutch were distinctly nervous. A 'summit' about the proposal meeting was held in Paris in February 1961 and again in Bonn in July that year: agreement was then reached on the creation of a special committee under the chairmanship of M. Christian Fouchet (then French ambassador to Denmark) to work out proposals to 'give shape to the desire for political union' (Bodenheimer, 1967; Silj, 1967).

That same month – July 1961 – Mr Macmillan announced to the House of Commons   55
his government's decision to apply for membership of the Community – a move which was shortly followed by formal application being lodged with the Community not only by Britain but also by Denmark, Ireland and Norway. The British had now realized that the dangers of remaining outside the Community – which showed at this stage every sign of success – outweighed the risks of joining. The attempt to exert pressure from outside through EFTA showed no sign of success and US support for the Six precluded any further attempts to press alternative strategies on the lines of the defunct European free trade area.

These developments seemed to underline the success of the Community and to offer   56
the prospect of it being expanded into a framework within which most of the countries of western Europe could move forward to more far-reaching economic and political integration.

7   Success, however, brought new tensions into the life of the Community which were   57
Conflict, crisis and to usher in a new and distinctly more troubled period in its development. The pro-
stagnation (1963–9) jected moves towards both geographical extension and political union failed, and although in the next six years the customs union was completed and some common policies agreed, the influence exerted by de Gaulle over its affairs during this period – and the hostility his policies aroused within it – eventually produced an impasse out of which the Community was only able to move after his departure from the French presidency in April 1969.

The first signs of major trouble appeared in the early part of 1962 when the negotia-   58
tions on political union ran into difficulties. In January that year a revised draft treaty was put forward by the French (apparently on the initiative of de Gaulle himself) to which several of the other members of the Community raised serious objections. Although none of them was prepared to put decision-making in such delicate areas of policy as defence and foreign affairs into the hands of a Commission, they were anxious both to safeguard the role of the existing Community institutions in the spheres covered by the three Treaties, and to make provision for a move towards at least some kind of Commission-type body after an initial three-year period. The institutions which de Gaulle proposed, on the other hand, were firmly intergovernmental in character: it was feared moreover that they would in practice tend to undermine the Commission in Brussels. The other members of the Community were also concerned about de Gaulle's attitude to NATO, and wished to have reassurance that the new Community organization would not weaken it, or lead to conflict with the United States.

The decisive opposition, however, came from the Dutch. They were anxious at all 59
costs to have the British by their side, believing that the interests of the two countries
were likely to be very close on all major issues, and fearing that otherwise they
might be squeezed between the French and the Germans. They argued that as
Britain was currently negotiating entry into the existing Communities she should
take part also in the talks on political union. The French refused: at which point
the Dutch effectively vetoed further negotiations within the Fouchet Committee.

This was no doubt a great relief to the British government which was having dif- 60
ficulty enough in convincing opinion in the country of the desirability of entry
without the additional complications that a new treaty would have brought. But
for de Gaulle it was further evidence of the dangers of allowing the British to join.
In January the following year, he, in turn, abruptly put an end to the negotiations
on entry. There can be little doubt that he did so primarily because of his wish to
exclude a potentially dangerous rival from the Community. At the time other
reasons were given, and in particular the 'non-European' character and interests
of Britain. This in his view had recently been demonstrated yet again by the outcome
of a meeting at Nassau between President Kennedy and Macmillan, at which the
US had offered Polaris missiles to the UK to replace Blue Streak. There was sufficient
truth in de Gaulle's argument for it to be effective with at least some sections of
opinion within the Six. Nevertheless de Gaulle had to be careful to ensure that in
saying no to the British he did not risk breaking up the Community itself.

The crucial element in the situation was the Federal Republic: had Adenauer sided 61
with the British, de Gaulle would have been virtually isolated. But in fact the Federal
Chancellor attached more importance to reconciliation with France: between de
Gaulle's press conference and the decisive meeting of the negotiators in Brussels he
went to Paris to sign a treaty of co-operation with France. This signalled the choice
he had made, and it meant that once the dust had settled the Federal Republic took
a leading part – together with the Commission – in urging that the Community
should continue towards the objectives set out in the Rome Treaties. There was

nevertheless a period of several months during which the other members of the Community showed their strong disapproval of de Gaulle's unilateral action by bringing the Brussels decision-making machinery to a halt. And although by mid-1963 a formula had been found to get it moving again, the French veto left a legacy of distrust among their partners which weighed heavily on subsequent developments. The style of bargaining changed, especially when after Adenauer's retirement from office later in 1963, de Gaulle found himself faced by an unsympathetic Chancellor in the person of Ludwig Erhard. For the latter the relationship with the United States was of capital importance, and he showed considerable support for the American proposal for a Multilateral Nuclear Force (MLF) within the framework of NATO which cut right across de Gaulle's attempts to get German support for the French *force de frappe*. De Gaulle retaliated by threatening to walk out of the Common Market unless the Germans agreed to the Commission's proposals for a common grain price, proposals which (the Commission argued) had to be settled before the Community could play a positive part in the mutual tariff-cutting negotiations which had been proposed by President Kennedy and which were due to take part within the framework of the General Agreement on Tariffs and Trade (GATT). The German interest in the success of these negotiations was substantial, as industry in the Federal Republic was anxious to obtain easier access to the US domestic market.

In December 1964 Erhard gave way, and agreement was reached on the level of the future common grain price. This was the first major decision reached by the Community since the collapse of the negotiations with Britain, and to some it seemed to usher in a new period of rapid forward movement. The Germans had also agreed to take part in work evolving a medium-term economic programme for the Community: a first modest step which the Commission hoped would lead beyond the customs union towards closer economic integration. Emboldened by these developments the Commission decided in the spring of 1965 to attempt to force the pace. It proposed that the terminal date for the customs union should be brought forward to 1 July 1967 to coincide with the coming into effect of common prices for agricultural products; that from the same date the Community should be financed directly from the proceeds of the Common External Tariff and the agricultural levies on imports of foodstuffs; and that some budgetary powers should be given to the European Parliament. 62

This was a bold package which aimed at strengthening the authority of the Commission and the Parliament at the same time as it pushed forward the process of economic integration. De Gaulle reacted angrily: to him it was a threat to the continued predominance of the national governments in the decision-making machinery of the Community. When his negotiators failed to 'untie' the package his response was to boycott the Community: and in the following months he widened his attack on the Commission which he scathingly dismissed as a group of *apatrides* (stateless persons). 63

For seven months the Community came to a virtually complete halt. Some routine business was transacted by correspondence, but otherwise there was complete paralysis. On this occasion de Gaulle was isolated, for although there were some differences among the other Five, they contrived to maintain a united front. In the December presidential election in France there was a significant volume of opposition to de Gaulle's European policy, and this may have contributed to his failure to win a clear majority on the first ballot. At all events, de Gaulle – who had already decided to withdraw French forces from the NATO command – now sought to withdraw from what had become a dangerously exposed position. At the end of January 1966, in Luxembourg, a compromise was reached. The institutional role of the Commission was confirmed (accompanied by a rather anodyne set of recommendations with regard to certain procedural aspects of its work), and the members 64

Ludwig Erhard, Chancellor of the Federal Republic of Germany. For him 'The relationship with the United States was of capital importance'

Georges Pompidou, President of France after de Gaulle. In 1969 he suggested a Summit meeting of the leaders of the Six

agreed to disagree about the use of majority voting in the Council of Ministers, France insisting that on matters of 'vital national importance', it would maintain a veto. At the same time the Commission's original package of measures was dropped.

The Luxembourg compromise while it blocked the institutional development of the 65 Community, also marked the end of de Gaulle's hopes of being able to shape it according to his wishes. For the time being a rather uneasy truce had been accepted by both sides, a truce which in May 1966 allowed the Council to fix 1 July 1968 as the date for the completion of the customs union and the common farm policy. But any hope of more far-reaching developments had to be indefinitely postponed (Newhouse, 1967).

It was in this situation that the Labour government in Britain decided to make a 66 second application to join. A majority of members in the cabinet had decided, like Mr Macmillan's government before them, that Britain was no longer able to sustain a world role on her own, and that the development of the Commonwealth did not offer a viable alternative. After a reconnaissance of the Community capitals early in 1967, the decision to apply was taken by the government and approved by an over-whelming majority in the House of Commons. This time, however, the negotiations did not even get to first base. In December, after another press conference given by the French President in which he made it clear that his objections to British entry remained, the Council of Ministers failed to agree on the British request for the opening of talks.

On this occasion, as in 1965, the French were isolated. And again the Five, backed 67 by the Commission, stood firm. A series of proposals were put forward with the aim of associating Britain with various aspects of the work of the Communities, and preparing the ground for later membership. Attempts were also made to revivify the Western European Union, and use this as a forum where issues of common foreign policy could be discussed with Britain: a move which led to conflict with France in that body, and its temporary withdrawal from active participation in it.

Although the Six were able to make some further progress in carrying out the 68
programme of work set out in the EEC treaty – the customs union, for instance, was
formally completed on 1 July 1968 as previously agreed,[5] and some advances were
made towards a common transport and foreign trade policy – disagreement over its
enlargement, and distrust of de Gaulle, cast a heavy shadow over its work. The
French President, for his part, while continuing to seek to extract the maximum of
economic benefit from the Community for France (particularly with regard to
agriculture) was casting around for some alternative political framework for
French policy. He courted the Soviet Union and a number of the east European
states on the one hand; on the other he began to toy with the idea of constructing a
new type of political directorate for western Europe with Britain, the Federal
Republic and Italy.

The British, however, maintained their application to join the existing Communities. 69
Relations with France became glacial as, together with the Five, they maintained
their pressure for the opening of negotiations. At this point an impasse had been
reached: it was only ended when de Gaulle resigned from the French presidency in
April 1969, having failed to obtain a majority in a referendum on a set of proposals
which included the abolition of the Senate and the creation of new regional
institutions in France.

Willi Brandt. As Chancellor of the Federal
Republic he believed that development of the
Communities provided the right framework
for Germany

Vicomte Davignon. The Davignon Committee
suggested twice yearly meetings of the Foreign
Ministers of the members of the Communities to
discuss foreign policy co-ordination

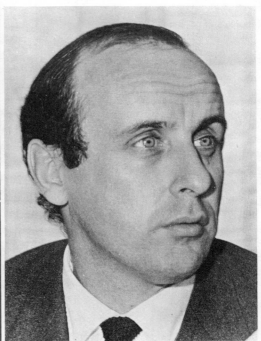

8
The second relance:
from The Hague to
the Paris Summit
(1969–72)
It took only a short time for the Community to regain its impetus. At the suggestion 70
of the new French President, Georges Pompidou, a summit meeting of the leaders of
the Six was held in The Hague in early December 1969 and there agreement was
reached on the outlines of a far-reaching programme for future action. This was
summed up in three words: completion, deepening and enlargement.

[5]This involved the final abolition of customs duties on goods traded within the Six, and the substitution of a
Common External Tariff towards the rest of the world for the previous separate national customs tariffs.

The new impetus derived from several sources. In the first place, there was the 71
desire of the new French government leaders to restore relations with their partners
in the Community. Although their policy statements retained a Gaullist intonation,
they were clearly anxious to break out of the isolation into which de Gaulle had led
the country. At the same time their willingness to open negotiations with Britain
suggested that they were beginning to feel uneasy about the economic and political
strength of the Federal Republic, and viewed British membership as providing a
guarantee against undue German influence in the Community. The Federal
Republic, for its part, now had a Chancellor – Willi Brandt – who was genuinely committed to furthering the economic and political development of the Community
which he believed provided the right framework for the Federal Republic, and a
necessary basis for its new *Ost-Politik* of seeking improved relations with the countries
of eastern Europe.

The Germans, for their part, came to the meeting determined as a first priority to 72
obtain agreement to the opening of negotiations with the applicant countries: the
French, on the other hand, appeared to give priority to the development of the
existing Community. A balance had therefore to be struck between the two, and
this was incorporated in the three-part package.

The first element in this was agreement on what was needed to be done to complete the 73
transition period as laid down in the EEC Treaty. The French insisted that an essential part of this was definitive arrangements for the financing of the Common
Agricultural Policy: it was agreed that these would be coupled with the direct
financing of the Community from its own resources rather than by annual grants
from national governments. Once agreement on this had been reached, the end of
the Community's transition period would be reached: in this sense, the initial tasks
laid down in the EEC treaty would have been completed.

But although the Community would have then reached its 'final stage' with the 74
coming into force of all the measures required for the establishment of the Common
Market, it was agreed that a series of further actions would be required to strengthen
the Community and promote its development into an economic union. This is what
was entailed by 'deepening'. The ministers agreed that in the first place during the
course of 1970 they would take decisions on proposals already presented by the
Commission for the achievement of an economic and monetary union. Other action
was to be taken to increase technological co-operation between the member countries, to give a new impetus to Euratom, to reform the Social Fund, and to renew
discussion on the establishment of a European university.

As far as enlargement was concerned, the ministers re-affiirmed their agreement in 75
principle that this should happen, and that negotiations should be opened with the
applicant states as well as with the other members of EFTA. Finally they added an
instruction to their foreign ministers 'to study the best way of achieving progress in
the matter of political unification, within the context of enlargement', and asked
them to report before the end of July 1970.

These decisions marked the opening of a new and much more creative phase in the 76
development of the Community. They opened up the twin prospects of geographical
enlargement and a far-reaching set of new objectives going well beyond the existing
treaties which were implied by economic and monetary union. Taken together these
made The Hague meeting at least as important as that held in Messina in 1955, and
showed, as that earlier meeting had also done, the extraordinary powers of recovery
of the Six after a period of frustration and disappointment.

Negotiations with the applicants were duly opened on 30 June 1970 in Luxembourg 77
with Britain, Denmark, Ireland and Norway. All the major issues in the British case
were settled within a year: astonishingly rapid progress in comparison with previous
attempts. In the meantime significant developments in other directions had also

taken place. Already in December 1970 the Council of Ministers agreed both on the final form of financing for the Common Agricultural Policy; the method by which the Community was to be financed by its own resources (primarily the proceeds of the external tariff and levies) and some budgetary powers for the European Parliament. In other words, they now settled the issues which had caused the crisis in 1965–6, and on lines not dissimilar from those originally proposed at that time by the Commission. As a result, the transition period of the EEC was formally ended on 31 December 1969, exactly twelve years after its establishment.

Progress towards economic and monetary union on the other hand proved much 78 more difficult. Early in 1970 steps were taken to strengthen the work being done on the elaboration of a medium-term economic programme, and agreement was reached on a short-term mutual aid system by which their central banks established a $2 billion fund to help each other in case of temporary balance of payments difficulties. In June the Council agreed in principle on the main recommendations of a committee set up under the Luxembourg Prime Minister, M. Pierre Werner, with regard to the achievement of economic and monetary union. They endorsed the view that this could be attained by 1980 'provided it enjoys the permanent political support of the governments', and that the first three-year stage towards it should open on 1 January 1971.

When it came to making more specific decisions on what exactly was to be done, 79 however, the ministers ran into difficulties. They were unable to agree in December 1970 on a formal commitment to 1980 as the target date for the achievement of economic and monetary union, the Germans and the Dutch stressing the importance of giving the Community greater powers for the effective co-ordination of national economic policies, while the French insisted on the importance of the prior co-ordination of some aspects of monetary policy and the need to concentrate on the steps needed for the first stage of the process. In February 1971, however, compromise was reached.

The ministers agreed: 80

a On a more detailed programme of work for the transition period to December 1972;
b To establish a fund with a ceiling of $2 billions and the necessary machinery to provide medium-term financial aid to members with balance of payment difficulties;
c To specify policy areas where some common action would be required including budgetary and taxation policy; internal monetary and credit policy; external monetary policy; a unified capital market; capital movements; and regional policy.

However they did not enter into a binding commitment to 1980 as the terminal date, 81 nor did they do more than indicate in the most general terms the machinery which economic and monetary union would require.

Hardly had these decisions been taken when expectations of a revaluation of the 82 DM caused a flow of 'hot' money into the Federal Republic, thus placing stress on the Community, and on the whole concept of monetary union. It was only after lengthy and heated debate that the Council of Ministers agreed to the German decision to let the mark float for a restricted period. This was, however, only a foretaste of worse to come.

The 'Smithsonian Agreement', reached in Washington in December 1971 – by 83 which exchange rates were realigned and the permissible margin of fluctuation of other currencies against the dollar widened from 2.25 to 4.5 per cent – was the resolution of a crisis begun in August following President Nixon's attempts to strengthen the dollar. The intervening months of intra-Community dissension on a common response to the crisis threatened to take the members further away from their own goal of narrower exchange rate margins.

The Six, together with Britain, attempted to counteract this in a series of moves in **84** March 1972 which were hailed as an important new step towards the goal of EMU. Fluctuations between Community currencies were limited to 2.25 per cent and measures were agreed to strengthen short-term economic co-ordination and to counteract regional disparities. However, the fragility of these attempts was made painfully apparent when in June Britain, Ireland and Denmark withdrew from their monetary commitment to the Community in order to float their currencies. Italy was also granted partial exception for three months.

During the same period only very cautious progress was made to the parallel goal of **85** political union – that is, measures to enable the Community to acquire a common foreign policy. Following The Hague Summit, a high-level committee of officials under a Belgian diplomat Vicomte Davignon was set up to review the situation and make proposals. But the report suggested only modest measures: twice-yearly meetings of foreign ministers to be serviced by quarterly meetings of a political committee consisting of senior foreign office officials. This was a far cry from the bolder proposals which had been considered in the early sixties at the time of the Fouchet negotiations. The new machinery was however set up, and the applicant countries also began to take an active part in its work.

As 1972 progressed attention was focused primarily on the preparations for a further **86** Summit meeting which, it was hoped, might list a new set of objectives for the enlarged Community. In an intensive series of discussions, which was pursued both at the level of heads of state and government and also in the Council of Ministers, general agreement emerged that there should be three main items on the agenda: economic and monetary union; political co-operation; and institutional questions. The preparation for the meeting, however, proved arduous. One major bone of contention was a French proposal that a political secretariat should be set up in Paris to promote foreign policy co-ordination. Once again fears were aroused that this might prove to be a device to by-pass the existing Community institutions, and at one stage disagreement on the issue seemed to threaten a postponement of the Summit.

In the end the issue was resolved by an agreement to drop the proposal, and the **87** Summit meeting duly took place in Paris on October 19/20.

The outcome of the meeting was a lengthy Communiqué which was a good deal more **88** positive than had been originally anticipated. It showed clearly that the Community had moved into a distinctly new phase of its evolution, not only in terms of its size,but also in terms of its ambitions. Two things were particularly striking about the preamble to the Communiqué: its emphasis on the role of the Community in the world at large, and the recognition of its authors that 'economic expansion is not an end in itself' and that in future the Community should pay far more attention to its social goals, including the quality of life to be achieved for its citizens. (The Communiqué is printed later in the unit – see pp. 78–81.)

This lengthy statement of future intentions was not achieved without a good deal **89** of hard bargaining, and it left most of the detail of future policies to be hammered out by the Community institutions. Nevertheless it was a comparatively clear statement of priorities for the future and an impressive confirmation that with enlargement a new impetus was given to the Community's search for 'a closer unity among the European peoples'.

In the meantime the Treaty of Accession had been submitted for approval both in the **90** existing member countries and the four applicant countries. Britain was the only one not to hold a referendum, the decision in favour of membership taking the form of the passage through Parliament of the European Communities Bill to give legal force to the Treaty. This was finally approved in the early autumn, in the face of strong opposition from a majority of the Labour party. By an overwhelming majority the Irish people approved of accession in a referendum held in May 1972; and the Danes by a majority of 63.5 per cent to 36.5 per cent. The Norwegians on the other hand rejected entry: the result of the referendum in that country produced a negative majority of 53 per cent to 47 per cent. As a result only three of the four intending new members ratified the Treaty of Accession, and the new Community which came into existence on 1 January 1973 has nine rather than ten members.

References

Bodenheimer, S. (1967) *Political Union, a Microcosm of European Politics*, Leyden, Sijthoff.

Camps, Miriam (1964) *Britain and the European Community, 1955–63*, London, Oxford University Press.

Diebold, William (1959) *Schuman Plan*, New York, Verry, Council on Foreign Relations Series.

Haas, Ernst B. (1968) *The unity of Europe* (2nd ed.), London, Oxford University Press.

Lerner, D. and Aron, R. (1957) *France Defeats the EDC*, New York, Praeger.

Lindberg, Leon (1963) *The Political Dynamics of European Economic Integration*, Stanford, Stanford University Press. (Quoting Walter Hallstein p. 273 – this study deals with EEC's activities in the period, 1958–62.)

Newhouse, John (1967) *Collision in Brussels*, London, Faber.

PEP (1968) *European unity, A survey of the European Organisations*, London, Political and Economic Planning. (For brief accounts of the work of the OEEC and the Council of Europe.)

Pryce, Roy (1962) *The Political Future of the European Community*, London, Marshbank/PEP. (For full text of statement by Mr Robert Schuman, 9 May 1950, see Appendix 1 of above.)

Ransom, Charles (1973) *The European Community and Eastern Europe*, London, Butterworths.

Silj, A. (1967) *Europe's political puzzle: a study of the Fouchet negotiations and the 1963 veto*, Cambridge, Mass., Harvard University Press.

Comments and questions

If you followed the suggestions at the beginning of this paper you should now have information organized in three ways:

a A list of the motives behind the movement towards European Unity. Compare this with your answers to Questions 8 and 10. How do the motives differ?

b A list of the major institutions with their initials. (You should also be able to say briefly what each one does.) Keep this for reference throughout the course.

c An annotated chronology for reference during the course.

Having studied this article you should be able to answer the questions below. (Refer back to the text if necessary.) Further comments on these questions are to be found in the Supplementary Material under 'Further Comments on Unit 1'. These comments draw your attention to points in the text and give suggestions for further thought.

12 Rank the following in order of importance in explaining the diminished faith in the nation state revealed in western Europe (Britain excluded) immediately after the Second World War.

    a The realization that in future individual states would not be able to control international business organizations.

    b The belief that nationalism had helped to cause two world wars.

    c The vulnerability of individual states to monetary and economic crises.

    d The realization that only by co-operation could western Europe gain an equal international voice with the USA and the USSR.

    e The inability revealed by individual nation states to defend themselves in time of war.

    f The need to co-operate for economic recovery.

13 In order to gain further insight into the motivation for European Unity attempt to reformulate in a few notes the reasons for the establishment and success of the ECSC given in this paper.

14 Which of the following statements would you accept about The Hague Summit Meeting of 1969?

    a It resolved the long-standing crisis caused by France's withdrawal in 1965.

    b It saw a major conflict between France and Germany on monetary matters.

    c It agreed that in future far greater attention would be paid to social goals, including the quality of individual life.

    d It agreed to reopen negotiations with applicant members.

    e It agreed to give greater emphasis to regional policy.

Further reading

Miriam Camps (1967) *European Unification in the Sixties*, London, Oxford University Press for the Royal Institute of International Affairs.

Ernst B. Haas (1968) *The Unity of Europe* (2nd ed.), London, Oxford University Press.

Leon Lindberg (1963) *The Political Dynamics of European Economic Integration*, Stanford, Stanford University Press.

Leon Lindberg and Stuart S. Scheingold (1970) *Europe's Would-Be-Polity*, New Jersey, Prentice-Hall.

Richard Mayne (1970) *The Recovery of Europe*, London, Weidenfeld and Nicholson.

Roy Pryce (1973) *The Politics of the European Community*, London, Butterworths.

F. R. Willis (1968) *France, Germany and the New Europe, 1945–1967* (2nd ed.), London, Oxford University Press.

F. R. Willis (1971) *Italy chooses Europe*, London, Blackwell/Oxford University Press.

Section 5
Conclusion to Unit 1 and self-assessment activities

Conclusion to Unit 1 and self-assessment activities

At the beginning of this unit on page 7, the course team set out what they considered were reasonable objectives to be achieved by the student while studying. Turn back to page 7 and remind yourself of these objectives. Ask yourself 'Can I do all these things?'.

You may have set yourself other personal objectives which you hoped to achieve by studying this unit. Have you achieved those also?

Having completed this week's work you should be able to answer the questions which follow and to do the activity suggested. Further comments which draw your attention to points in the text and give suggestions for further thought are to be found in the Supplementary Material under 'Further comments on Unit 1'.

15 Turn back to page 10. If you were unable to complete all these questions before you started the course, answer them now.

16 Which among the following have been important motives furthering western European integration. For those you identify as important motives state whether they would be given greater emphasis in 1950 or 1970:

   a A more even spread of individual wealth;

   b Stimulate economic growth;

   c Protection of the environment;

   d Counter any future military threat from Germany;

   e Encourage American economic support;

   f Counter American economic domination;

   g Oppose communist expansion.

17 Note down about half a dozen points made by Mr Heath and Sir Alec Douglas-Home in favour of British entry into the EEC. (See 'The Great Debate' in the Reader). And then note a similar number of points made against entry at that time by Mr Wilson and Mr Healey. Then, on the basis of your reading so far, note against each point whether you think it has so far: (a) proved right; (b) proved wrong; (c) partly right/partly wrong; or (d) too early to judge.

18 Questions for discussion.

   18.1 The Paris Summit Communiqué records:

   The member states of the Community, the driving force of European construction, affirm their intention before the end of the present decade to transform the whole complex of their relations into a European union.

   This is an example of a 'diplomatic' style of writing. What do you think it means?

   18.2 The British government refused to be involved in the foundation of the EEC, yet a few years later it applied for entry, and this application was repeated by two subsequent administrations. Identify the main reasons for this change of attitude, and for the persistence of the attempts to join after the first failure.

Section 6
Reference reading

Contents

Chronology of Events in the Formation of the European Communities
Compiled for the Course Team by Gail Price

1946   Sept.   Churchill's speech at Zurich urges Franco-German reconciliation within a kind of 'United States of Europe'.

1947   June   General Marshall proposes American aid to stimulate European recovery – European Payments Union (EPU) to distribute this.

                Oct.   Creation of Benelux – economic union of Belgium, the Netherlands and Luxembourg.

1948   March   Brussels Treaty – Benelux, France and England.

                April   OEEC (Organization for European Economic Co-operation) formed from the Committee for European Economic Co-operation, formerly set up by 16 countries to assess their requirements in goods and foreign exchange for 1948–52.

1949   April   North Atlantic Treaty Organization (NATO) formed by 12 states for defence purposes.

                May   Statute of Council of Europe signed – 5 Brussels Treaty Powers + Sweden, Denmark, Eire, Norway and Italy, and soon after, Iceland, Greece, Turkey, W. Germany and Austria. It was to be a forum of opinion for Western European parliamentarians, but could not bring about political unity as hoped. The governments had given it no real powers, although it had wide terms of reference. Decisions subject to veto.

1950   May   Schuman Plan – proposal to place French and German coal and steel under a common authority.

                         European Defence Community plan devised and presented by René Pleven, French Defence Minister. The plan was to integrate Germany into the defence of western Europe. After four years of debate it was rejected by the French National Assembly.

1951   April   European Coal and Steel Community (ECSC) Treaty signed by the Six – Benelux, France, Germany and Italy – 'to establish, by creating an economic community, the foundation of a wider and deeper community'. To become operational in 1953. Set up the first common European authority – the ECSC High Authority, subject to democratic control through an Assembly composed of representatives from six national parliaments, and to rule of law through the Court of Justice.

1954   Oct.   Western European Union (WEU) formed – the Six + Britain – the military response to the collapse of the EDC, but did not advance functional and economic integration.

                Dec.   UK Association agreement with ECSC.

1955   June   Messina Conference of the Foreign Ministers of the Six, set up a Committee under Paul-Henri Spaak to study ways in which 'a fresh advance towards the building of Europe' could be achieved.

1957   March   Rome Treaties signed, setting up European Economic Community (EEC) and Euratom – the Six.

1958	Jan.	Rome Treaties come into effect.
1959	Nov.	European Free Trade Association (EFTA) formed by Austria, Denmark, Norway, Sweden, Switzerland, Portugal and the UK.
1961	July	Association Agreement with Greece.
	Aug.	Ireland applies for membership. Denmark and UK request negotiations aimed at membership.
1962	Jan.	Basic features of Common Agricultural Policy (CAP) agreed.
	March	UK applies for membership.
	April	Norway requests negotiations for membership.
1963	Jan.	Negotiations to extend membership broken off after de Gaulle's speech vetoing British entry. Signing of Franco-German Friendship Treaty.
	July	Yaoundé Convention signed – Association of 18 African States and Madagascar with the Community for five years.
	Sept.	Association Agreement signed with Turkey and Trade Agreement with Iran.
1964	June	Yaoundé Convention comes into force.
1965	July	Council fails to reach agreement on financing CAP. French boycott of Community institutions for seven months in opposition to Commission proposal that all import duties and levies be paid in to the Community budget, and the powers of the European Parliament be increased.
1966	Jan.	Foreign Ministers of the Six reach a compromise and agree to resume full activities of the Community.
	July	Association Agreement signed with Nigeria.
	Nov.	British Prime Minister Harold Wilson announces plan for 'high level approach' to the Six, with intention of applying for membership.
1967	May	Britain, Ireland and Denmark submit formal applications for membership.
	July	Community Executives merged into one 14-man Commission.
	Dec.	Council reaches deadlock over enlargement after General de Gaulle objects to UK entry.
1968	July	Customs Union completed – Common External Tariff operates around the Common Market. The Six adopt basic regulations for a common transport policy. Arusha Convention – Association Agreement with Kenya, Uganda and Tanzania. The Six remove remaining restrictions on free movement of workers.
	Dec.	The Mansholt Plan for agriculture announced – a radical 10 year reform programme.

1969	April	Resignation of General de Gaulle.
	July	M. Pompidou elected President of France. 'Yaoundé II' signed – regulates trade and aid relations until 1975.
	Sept.	Partial Association Agreements with Morocco and Tunisia.
	Dec.	Hague Summit – the Six agree to complete, enlarge and strengthen the Community. The Council agrees to finance CAP, giving the Community its own resources from 1978 and strengthening the Europe Parliament's budgetary powers.
1970	Feb.	UK white paper on benefits of EEC membership.
	March	Three-year non-preferential agreement with Yugoslavia signed.
	June	1980 set as target date for Economic and Monetary Union (EMU).
	July	Davignon Report – advocates twice yearly ministerial meetings on political co-operation. Opening of enlargement negotiations.
	Oct.	Trade Agreements with Israel and Spain signed.
1971	Feb.	Common Fisheries Policy takes effect.
	April	Association Agreement with Malta operational.
	May	Heath–Pompidou Summit paves way to agreement in enlargement negotiations.
	June	Agreement reached on Britain's entry to EEC.
	Oct.	British House of Commons votes to join EEC on terms secured.
1972	Jan.	Treaty of Accession signed by Denmark, Ireland, Norway and UK.
	Sept.	Norwegian referendum shows majority against entry. Norway withdraws.
	Oct.	Paris Summit of the Nine prepares a blueprint for the future development of the Community.
1973	Jan.	Denmark, Ireland and UK join the Community – the Six become the Nine.

A glossary of Western European organizations
Compiled for the Course Team by Robert Masterton

Membership of Western Organizations – January 1973

Countries	OECD	NATO	Council of Europe	WEU	ECSC	EEC	EUR-ATOM	EFTA
					European Communities			
Australia	×							
Belgium	×	×	×	×	×	×	×	
France	×	×	×	×	×	×	×	
Germany	×	×	×	×	×	×	×	
Italy	×	×	×	×	×	×	×	
Luxembourg	×	×	×	×	×	×	×	
Netherlands	×	×	×	×	×	×	×	
Austria	×		×					×
Canada	×	×						
Cyprus			×					
Denmark	×	×	×		×	×	×	
Finland	×							A
Greece	×	×				A		
Iceland	×	×	×					×
Eire	×		×		×	×	×	
Japan	×							
Malta			×			A		
Norway	×	×	×					×
Portugal	×	×						×
Spain	×							
Sweden	×		×					×
Switzerland	×		×					×
Turkey	×	×	×			A		
United Kingdom	×	×	×	×	×	×	××	
United States	×	×						
Yugoslavia	+							

Key to chart:

× = Member

+ = Yugoslavia has special status in OECD

A = Associate

Council of Europe

The Council of Europe was set up on 5 May, 1949, 'to achieve a greater unity between its members for the purpose of safeguarding and realizing the ideals and principles which are their common heritage and facilitating their economic and social progress'.

With 17 countries the Council has the widest membership among European organizations. Membership is restricted to parliamentary democracies but most of the Council's activities are open to non-member states. The organization is composed of a Committee of Ministers, in which agreements are reached on common action by governments, and a 140-strong Assembly, which makes proposals for new activities and serves, more generally, as a parliamentary forum for Europe. The Council employs an international staff of 650.

Over 70 intergovernmental Conventions and Agreements have been concluded by the Council, chief among which are the Convention on Human Rights and the Social Charter. The organization further promotes on-going co-operation to improve education, the safeguarding of the urban and natural environment, social services, public health, the protection of consumers and the harmonization of law throughout Europe. The Council's overall aim is to maintain and enhance the quality of life for the 300 million citizens of its member states.

Address for further information:
Directorate of Press and Information, Council of Europe, 67-Strasbourg, France.

EFTA (European Free Trade Association)

EFTA was brought into existence in May 1960 on the basis of the Stockholm Convention of 1959. It was made up of eight member countries (Austria, Denmark, Iceland, Norway, Portugal, Sweden, Switzerland, United Kingdom) and one associate (Finland).

Its two objectives were, first to establish, by annual steps, free trade in industrial products between the member countries and to promote trade in agricultural goods, and secondly, to make western Europe a single market for industrial goods.

All tariffs and quotas on industrial trade between the members were abolished by the end of 1966, and by Finland a year later. EFTA also abolished a large number of non-tariff barriers. The trade effects were an almost four-fold increase in intra-EFTA exports, against a background of a two-and-a-half times increase in total EFTA exports to the world.

The second EFTA objective is also in sight. As Britain and Denmark have joined the EEC, so the other members of EFTA have negotiated special relationships based on eventual free trade in industrial goods.

EFTA is directed by a Council, meeting weekly at the level of Ambassadors and twice yearly at Ministerial level. The Council is served by a secretariat in its Geneva headquarters and has several standing committees as well as a considerable number of *ad hoc* working parties.

Address for further information:
EFTA Information Department, 9, Rue Varembé, 1211 Geneva 20, Switzerland.

OECD (Organization for Economic Co-operation and Development)

The OEEC – Organization for European Economic Co-operation – was set up in 1948 to administer Marshall Plan aid and the co-operative effort of European recovery from the economic disaster of the Second World War.

On 14 December 1960 eighteen European countries together with Canada and the United States signed a convention to replace the purely European OEEC with a new organization. The convention came into force on 30 September 1961 when OEEC was superseded by the new organization, OECD, which now has a world-wide membership.

OECD aims at achieving the highest sustainable economic growth, full employment and a rising standard of living in member countries. It also contributes to economic expansion in member and non-member countries in the process of economic development.

To carry out these aims OECD has as its three main tasks:

1 Economic policy co-ordination;

2 Expansion of trade;

3 Aid to developing countries.

OECD does not itself give aid, but promotes increased and improved assistance efforts by its members.

OECD also deals with the more specialized considerations of the environment, manpower and social affairs, science and education, industry, agriculture and fisheries, and the peaceful uses of nuclear energy.

Address for further information:

OECD Information Service, 2, rue André-Pascal, 75 Paris 16, France.

WEU (Western European Union)

This seven-member organization grew out of the five-member Brussels Treaty Organization founded in March 1948 by Belgium, France, Luxembourg, the Netherlands and the United Kingdom. After the Paris Agreements of 1954, which revised the Brussels Treaty and extended it to include Western Germany and Italy, the Brussels Treaty Organization became Western European Union.

The WEU has a Council, normally of the seven Foreign Ministers, which makes an annual report to the WEU Assembly composed of the representatives from the WEU countries attending the Consultative Assembly of the Council of Europe. This Assembly holds debates on the state of European defence and on the activities of the WEU Council and its agencies, which include an Agency for the Control of Armaments and a standing Armaments Committee.

Since 1963 the WEU Council has held regular quarterly sessions at Ministerial level for political consultation and to exchange views on the European economic situation. Representatives of the EEC Commission participate in the economic discussion.

Address for further information:

8/9 Grosvenor Place, London, SW1.

NATO (North Atlantic Treaty Organization)

The North Atlantic Treaty was signed in Washington DC on 4 April 1949. It associates Britain and twelve other European countries with Canada and the United States of America in an alliance whose purpose is 'to safeguard the freedom, common heritage and civilization of their peoples, founded on the principles of democracy, individual liberty and the rule of law'.

The intention of NATO is the defence of its members by ensuring that third parties understand their collective determination to resist agression.

Although defence has priority, the fifteen member Governments co-operate in NATO on a variety of political, economic, scientific and environmental affairs. NATO decisions are reached by unanimous agreement among the representatives of the fifteen governments who comprise the North Atlantic Council, to which both the civilian and military branches are subordinate. Although there is no parliamentary assembly a conference of parliamentarians from NATO countries meets annually.

Address for further information:

NATO Information Service, NATO/OTAN, Brussels 1110, Belgium.

The Communique of the Paris Summit, October 1972
Introduced by Roy Pryce

The Communiqué of the Paris Summit showed clearly that the Community had moved into a distinctly new phase of its evolution, not only in terms of its size, but also in terms of its ambitions. Two things were particularly striking about the preamble to the Communiqué: its emphasis on the role of the Community in the world at large, and the recognition of its authors that 'economic expansion is not an end in itself' and that in future the Community should pay far more attention to its social goals, including the quality of life to be achieved for its citizens.

The detailed substantive part of the Communiqué then reviewed the major areas of the future work of the Community, which it said should aim to transform itself, before the end of the decade, into a 'European union'. Pride of place among the specific objectives to be achieved within this framework was given to economic and monetary union, the terminal date for which was confirmed as being not later than the end of 1980. Steps were to be taken during the course of 1973 to enable transition to the second stage of this union on 1 January 1974: these were to include the setting up of a European Monetary Co-operation Fund, to be administered by the Committee of the Central Banks of the Community countries; concerted action to narrow exchange rate fluctuations; the creation of a European monetary unit of account; and new measures for short-term monetary support. Parallel with these measures, further measures were to be taken to strengthen and intensify the co-ordination of economic policies, with priority being given to the fight against inflation. It was also agreed that the Community should take up a common position on international monetary issues and seek a reform of the existing system, the criteria for which were also specified in the Communiqué.

A new emphasis was also given by the meeting to the regional policy – on which Mr Heath has laid particular insistence. It was agreed that the Commission should be asked to prepare a report on the situation and to formulate specific proposals; that the member governments would in future co-ordinate their national policies, and that at the Community level a Regional Development Fund would be established before the end of 1973, to be financed from Community funds in the second stage of the transition towards economic and monetary union. Its terms of reference would cover not only help for agricultural regions but those suffering from 'industrial change and structural underemployment'.

Further sections of the Communiqué dealt with the social, industrial (including scientific and technological policy), environmental and energy policies, with a set of timetables for action specified in each case. With regard to the Community's external relations the section devoted to the developing countries struck a careful balance between French and British interests in its statement that 'the Community must, without detracting from the advantages enjoyed by countries with which it has special relations, respond even more than in the past to the expectations of all the developing countries'. It also emphasized (no doubt at French insistence) 'the essential importance' which it attached to the association agreements and Mediterranean policy – while adding references to its UNCTAD-inspired scheme [United Nations Conference on Aid and Development] of generalized preferences, market stabilization schemes for primary products and an (unspecified) increase in government aid to the developing world. All these matters, the Communiqué added, would be the subject of studies and decisions 'in good time' during 1973.

With regard to other aspects of its foreign trade policy the Summit made particularly reference to the United States, Canada and Japan with whom it said it was anxious to maintain 'a constructive dialogue'. It also committed the Community to making decisions on a global approach to all aspects of foreign trade policy by the middle of 1973, and to participate in the new round of negotiations being proposed within the framework of the General Agreement on Tariffs and Trade (GATT). It also reaffirmed the Community's intention of following a common commercial policy towards the countries of eastern Europe from 1 January 1973.

On the more specifically political aspects of external relations, the Summit called on its members to make 'a concerted and constructive contribution' to the Conference on Security and Co-operation in Europe; agreed that in future its foreign ministers would meet four times a year (rather than twice as in the past) to further co-ordination of their policies in this sphere, and that by mid-1973 they would present a report on how their co-operation could be further improved.

The two final sections of the Communiqué deal respectively with institutional reform and the achievement of a 'European union' – both in notably generalized terms. Any significant institutional reform (other than an agreement that in future national cabinet meetings should be held on the same day of the week) was in fact postponed – in spite of Dutch insistence that a firm date should be fixed for the introduction of direct elections to the European Parliament. Instead the Commission was asked to submit proposals for changes before 1 May 1973, and the ministers undertook to take decisions before the end of the first stage of the transitional period for economic and monetary union. But no specific reforms were mentioned nor were any specific dates fixed for their introduction. A rather ambiguous paragraph invited the Commission and the Council to take some practical steps to strengthen the powers of the Parliament and to improve their own relations with it, without indicating what precisely was to be done. Similarly the notion of the projected 'European union' was not spelled out, though it was agreed that a report on it would be drawn up before the end of 1975 for submission to a new Summit meeting.

A 'European union' by 1980

The Communiqué issued by the Nine after their summit conference in Paris on 19-20 October 1972

The heads of state or of government of the countries of the enlarged Community, meeting for the first time on 19 and 20 October in Paris, at the invitation of the President of the French Republic, solemnly declare:

At the moment when enlargement, decided in accordance with the rules in the Treaties and with respect for what the six original member states have already achieved, is to become a reality and to give a new dimension to the Community;

At a time when world events are profoundly changing the international situation;

Now that there is a general desire for détente and co-operation in response to the interest and the wishes of all peoples;

Now that serious monetary and trade problems require a search for lasting solutions that will favour growth with stability;

Now that many developing countries see the gap widening between themselves and the industrial nations and claim with justification an increase in aid and a fairer use of wealth;

Now that the tasks of the Community are growing, and fresh responsibilities are being laid upon it, the time has come for Europe to recognize clearly the unity of its interests, the extent of its capacities and the magnitude of its duties; Europe must be able to make its voice heard in world affairs, and to make an original contribution commensurate with its human intellectual and material resources. It must affirm its own views in international relations as befits its mission to be open to the world and for progress, peace and co-operation.

To this end:

i   The member states reaffirm their determination to base the development of their Community on democracy, freedom of opinion, the free movement of people and of ideas and participation by their peoples through their freely elected representatives;

ii   The member states are determined to strengthen the Community by establishing an economic and monetary union, the guarantee of stability and growth, the foundation of their solidarity and the indispensable basis for social progress, and by ending disparities between the regions;

iii   Economic expansion is not an end in itself. Its firm aim should be to enable disparities in living conditions to be reduced. It must take place with the participation of all the social partners. It should result in an improvement in the quality of life as well as in standards of living. As befits the genius of Europe, particular attention will be given to intangible values and to protecting the environment, so that progress may really be put at the service of mankind;

iv   The Community is well aware of the problem presented by continuing underdevelopment in the world. It affirms its determination, within the framework of a worldwide policy towards the developing countries, to increase its effort in aid and technical assistance to the least favoured people. It will take particular account of the concerns of those countries towards which, through geography, history and the commitments entered into by the Community, it has specific responsibilities;

v   The Community reaffirms its determination to encourage the development of international trade. This determination applies to all countries without exception.

The Community is ready to participate, as soon as possible, in the open-minded spirit that it has already shown, and according to the procedures laid down by the IMF [International Monetary Fund] and the GATT [General Agreement on Tariffs and Trade] in negotiations based on the principle of reciprocity. These should make it possible to establish, in the monetary and commercial fields, stable and balanced economic relations, in which the interests of the developing countries must be taken fully into account;

vi   The member states of the Community, in the interests of good neighbourly relations which should exist among all European countries whatever their regime, affirm their determination to pursue their policy of détente and of peace with the countries of Eastern Europe, notably on the occasion of the conference on security and co-operation in Europe, and the establishment on a sound basis of a wider economic and human co-operation;

vii   The construction of Europe will allow it, in conformity with its ultimate political objectives, to affirm its personality while remaining faithful to its traditional friendships and to the alliances of the member states, and to establish its position in world affairs as a distinct entity determined to promote a better international equilibrium, respecting the principles of the Charter of the United Nations. The member states of the Community, the driving force of European construction, affirm their intention to transform before the end of the present decade the whole complex of their relations into a European union.

Economic and monetary questions

1   The heads of state or of government reaffirm the determination of the member states of the enlarged European Communities irreversibly to achieve the economic and monetary union, confirming all the elements of the instruments adopted by the Council and by the representatives of member states on 22 March, 1971, and 21 March, 1972.

The necessary decisions should be taken in the course of 1973 so as to allow the transition to the second stage of the economic and monetary union on 1 January, 1974, and with a view to its completion not later than 31 December, 1980.

The heads of state or government reaffirmed the principle of parallel progress in the different fields of the economic and monetary union.

2 They declared that fixed but adjustable parities between their currencies constitute an essential basis for the achievement of the union and expressed their determination to set up within the Community mechanisms for defence and mutual support which would enable member states to ensure that they are respected.

They decided to institute before 1 April, 1973, by solemn instrument, based on the EEC Treaty, a European Monetary Co-operation Fund which will be administered by the Committee of Governors of Central Banks within the context of general guidelines on economic policy laid down by the Council of Ministers. In an initial phase the fund will operate on the following bases:

Concerted action among the central banks for the purposes of narrowing the margins of fluctuation between their currencies;

The multilateralization of positions resulting from interventions in Community currencies and the multi-lateralization of intra-Community settlements;

The use for this purpose of a European monetary unit of account;

The administration of short-term monetary support among the central banks;

The very short-term financing of the agreement on the narrowing of margins and short-term monetary support will be regrouped in the fund under renovated mechanism; to this end, short-term support will be adjusted on the technical plane without modifying its essential characteristics and in particular without modifying the consultation procedures they involve.

The competent bodies of the Community shall submit reports:

Not later than 30 September, 1973, on the adjustment of short-term support;

Not later than 31 December, 1973, on the conditions for the progressive pooling of reserves.

3 The heads of state or of government stressed the need to co-ordinate more closely the economic policies of the Community and for this purpose to introduce more effective Community procedures.

Under existing economic conditions they consider that priority should be given to the fight against inflation and to a return to price stability. They instructed their competent ministers to adopt, on the occasion of the enlarged Council of 30 and 31 October, 1972, precise measures in the various fields which lend themselves to effective and realistic short-term action towards these objectives and which take account of the respective situations of the countries of the enlarged Community.

4 The heads of state or of government express their determination that the member states of the enlarged Community should contribute by a common attitude to directing the reform of the international monetary system towards the introduction of an equitable and durable order.

They consider that this system should be based on the following principles:

Fixed but adjustable parities;

The general convertibility of currencies;

Effective international regulation of the world supply of liquidities;

A reduction in the role of national currencies as reserve instruments;

The effective and equitable functioning of the adjustment process;

Equal rights and duties for all participants in the system;

The need to lessen the unstabilizing effects of short-term capital movements;

The taking into account of the interests of the developing countries.

Such a system would be fully compatible with the achievement of the economic and monetary union.

Regional policy

5 The heads of state or of government agreed that a high priority should be given to the aim of correcting, in the Community, the structural and regional imbalances which might affect the realization of economic and monetary union.

The heads of state or of government invite the Commission to prepare without delay a report analysing the regional problems which arise in the enlarged Community and to put forward appropriate proposals.

From now on they undertake to co-ordinate their regional policies. Desirous of directing that effort towards finding a Community solution to regional problems, they invite the Community institutions to create a Regional Development Fund. This will be set up before 31 December, 1973, and will be financed, from the beginning of the second phase of economic and monetary union, from the Community's own resources. Intervention by the fund in co-ordination with national aids should permit, progressively with the realization of economic and monetary union, the correction of the main regional imbalances in the enlarged Community and particularly those resulting from the preponderance of agriculture and from industrial change and structural underemployment.

Social policy

6 The heads of state or heads of government emphasized that they attached as much importance to vigorous action in the social field as to the achievement of the economic and monetary union. They thought it essential to ensure the increasing involvement of labour and management in the economic and social decisions of the Community. They invited the institutions, after consulting labour and management, to draw up, between now and 1 January, 1974, a programme of action providing for concrete measures and the corresponding resources particularly in the framework of the Social Fund, based on the suggestions made in the course of the conference by heads of state and heads of government and by the Commission.

This programme should aim, in particular, at carrying out a co-ordinated policy for employment and vocational training, at improving working conditions and conditions of life, at closely involving workers in the progress of firms, at facilitating on the basis of the situation in the different countries the conclusion of collective agreements at European level in appropriate fields and at strengthening and co-ordinating measures of consumer protection.

Industrial, scientific and technological policy

7　The heads of state or of government consider it necessary to seek to establish a single industrial base for the Community as a whole.

This involves the elimination of technical barriers to trade as well as the elimination, particularly in the fiscal and legal fields, of barriers which hinder closer relations and mergers between firms, the rapid adoption of a European company statute, the progressive and effective opening up of public sector purchases, the promotion on a European scale of competitive firms in the field of high technology, the transformation and conversion of declining industries, under acceptable social conditions, the formulation of measures to ensure that mergers affecting firms established in the Community are in harmony with the economic and social aims of the Community, and the maintenance of fair competition as much within the Common Market as in external markets in conformity with the rules laid down by the Treaties.

Objectives will need to be defined and the development of a common policy in the field of science and technology ensured. This policy will require the co-ordination, within the institutions of the Community, of national policies and joint implementation of projects of interest to the Community.

To this end, a programme of action together with a precise timetable and appropriate measures should be decided by the Community's institutions, before 1 January, 1974.

Environment policy

8　The heads of state or of government emphasized the importance of a Community environmental policy. To this end they invited the Community institutions to establish, before 31 July, 1973, a programme of action accompanied by a precise timetable.

Energy policy

9　The heads of state and heads of government deem it necessary to invite the Community institutions to formulate as soon as possible an energy policy guaranteeing certain and lasting supplies under satisfactory economic conditions.

External relations

10　The heads of state or of government affirm that their efforts to construct their Community attain their full meaning only in so far as member states succeed in acting together to cope with the growing world responsibilities incumbent on Europe.

11　The heads of state or of government are convinced that the Community must, without detracting from the advantages enjoyed by countries with which it has special relations, respond even more than in the past to the expectations of all the developing countries.

With this in view, it attaches essential importance to the policy of association as confirmed in the Treaty of Accession and to the fulfilment of its commitments to the countries of the Mediterranean basin with which agreements have been or will be concluded, agreements which should be the subject of an overall and balanced approach.

In the same perspective, in the light of the results of the UNCTAD [United Nations Conference on Trade and Development] conference and in the context of the development strategy adopted by the United Nations, the institutions of the Community and member states are invited progressively to adopt an overall policy of development co-operation on a worldwide scale, comprising, in particular, the following elements:

The promotion in appropriate cases of agreements concerning the primary products of the developing countries with a view to arriving at market stabilization and an increase in their exports;

The improvement of generalized preferences with the aim of achieving a steady increase in imports of manufactures from the developing countries;

In this connection the Community institutions will study from the beginning of 1973 the conditions which will permit the achievement of a substantial growth target.

An increase in the volume of official financial aid.

An improvement in the financial conditions of this aid, particularly in favour of the least developed countries, bearing in mind the recommendations of the OECD [Organization for Economic Co-operation and Development] development assistance committee.

These questions will be the subject of studies and decisions in good time during 1973.

12　With regard to the industrial countries, the Community is determined, in order to ensure the harmonious development of world trade:

To contribute, while respecting what has been achieved by the Community, to a progressive liberalization of international trade by measures based on reciprocity and relating to both tariffs and non-tariff barriers;

To maintain a constructive dialogue with the United States, Japan, Canada and its other industrialized trade partners in a forthcoming spirit, using the most appropriate methods.

In this context the Community attaches major importance to the multilateral negotiations in the context of GATT which it will participate in, in accordance with its earlier statement.

To this end, the Community institutions are invited to decide not later than 1 July, 1973, on a global approach covering all aspects affecting trade.

The Community hopes that an effort on the part of all partners will allow these negotiations to be completed in 1975.

It confirms its desire for the full participation of the developing countries in the preparation and progress of these negotiations which should take due account of the interests of those countries.

Furthermore, having regard to the agreements concluded with the EFTA [European Free Trade Association] countries which are not members, the Community declares its readiness to seek with Norway a speedy solution to the trade problems facing that country in its relations with the enlarged Community.

13 In order to promote détente in Europe, the conference reaffirmed its determination to follow a common commercial policy towards the countries of Eastern Europe with effect from 1 January, 1973; member states declared their determination to promote a policy of co-operation, founded on reciprocity, with these countries.

This policy of co-operation is, at the present stage, closely linked with the preparation and progress of the conference on security and co-operation in Europe to which the enlarged Community and its member states are called upon to make a concerted and constructive contribution.

14 The heads of state or of government agreed that political co-operation between the member states of the Community on foreign policy matters had begun well and should be still further improved. They agreed that consultations should be intensified at all levels and that the Foreign Ministers should in future meet four times a year instead of twice for this purpose. They considered that the aim of their co-operation was to deal with problems of current interest and, where possible, to formulate common medium- and long-term positions, keeping in mind, inter alia, the international political implications for and effects of Community policies under construction. On matters which have a direct bearing on Community activities, close contact will be maintained with the institutions of the Community. They agreed that the Foreign Ministers should produce, not later than 30 June, 1973, a second report on methods of improving political co-operation in accordance with the Luxembourg report.

Reinforcement of institutions

15 The heads of state or government recognized that the structures of the Community had proved themselves, though they felt that the decision-making procedures and the functioning of the institutions should be improved, in order to make them more effective.

The Community institutions and, where appropriate, the representatives of the governments of member states are invited to decide before the end of the first stage in the achievement of the economic and monetary union, on the basis of the report which the Commission, pursuant to the resolution of 22 March, 1971, is to submit before 1 May, 1973, on the measures relating to the distribution of competences and responsibilities among the Community institutions and member states which are necessary to the proper functioning of an economic and monetary union.

They felt it desirable that the date on which meetings of national cabinets were normally held should be the same so that the Council of the Communities could organize itself with a more regular timetable.

Desiring to strengthen the powers of control of the European Parliamentary Assembly, independently of the date on which it will be elected by universal suffrage under Article 138 of the Treaty of Rome, and to make their contribution towards improving its working conditions, the heads of state or government, while confirming the decision of 22 April, 1970, of the Council of the Communities, invited the Council and the Commission to put into effect without delay the practical measures designed to achieve this reinforcement and to improve the relations both of the Council and of the Commission with the Assembly.

The Council will, before 30 June, 1973, take practical steps to improve its decision-making procedures and the cohesion of Community action.

They invited the Community institutions to recognize the right of the Economic and Social Committee in future to advise on its own initiative on all questions affecting the Community.

They were agreed in thinking that, for the purpose in particular of carrying out the tasks laid down in the different programmes of action, it was desirable to make the widest possible use of all the dispositions of the treaties, including Article 235 of the EEC Treaty.

European union

16 The heads of state or government, having set themselves the major objective of transforming, before the end of the present decade and with the fullest respect for the treaties already signed, the whole complex of the relations of member states into a European Union, request the institutions of the Community to draw up a report on this subject before the end of 1975 for submission to a summit conference.

Why join the Common Market?

Your Questions Answered

THE COMMON MARKET SAFEGUARD CAMPAIGN, 55 PARK LANE, LONDON, W.1. 01-629 8741

1. WOULD BRITAIN SUFFER LOSS OF SOVEREIGNTY AS A MEMBER OF THE COMMON MARKET?

Yes. Under the Treaty of Rome, Common Market Law and practice would replace our national law and practice over a wide range of economic and social life. Regulations made in Brussels would apply directly in Britain, and would have the force of law. Our Parliament would be powerless to modify them. Parliament would no longer be the sole law-making agency in Britain, and we would have to commit ourselves to accept and apply Common Market law in all matters covered by the Treaty, whether Parliament wished it or not. This surrender of our rights to make our own decisions in our domestic affairs would be for ever, as the Treaty imposes obligations in perpetuity and cannot be terminated by notice like other Treaties. These are the immediate, automatic and minimum consequences of signing the Treaty of Rome.

2. WOULD BRITAIN LOSE HER NATIONAL INDEPENDENCE?

Yes, almost certainly before long. The Common Market is already committed to introducing in the future a Common Currency and a directly-elected Parliament. The financial regulations already agreed by the Six will impose a Federal-style budget by 1980. All this must mean that a central Common Market Government would be established; and the member countries, including Britain, would be reduced to the status of mere States or provinces, like Ohio or Pennsylvania in the U.S. In these circumstances, Britain would cease to be an independent sovereign State, and the power to recover the right of self-Government would be irrevocably taken out of the hands of the British people. This would be a surrender totally different in principle from the limited and reversible sacrifice of rights accepted in a normal Treaty.

3. HOW MUCH WOULD FOOD PRICES RISE IN BRITAIN IF WE JOINED THE COMMON MARKET?

By 4s. or 5s. in the £ permanently. A family now spending £10 a week on food would have to spend £12–£12. 10s. a week to buy the same food. *Meat would cost 3s. or 4s. a lb. more, butter 5s. or 6s. more and cheese 3s. more.* Sugar would go up by about one half in price, and bread by about one third. Old people and large families would be cruelly hit. These rises would be *additional* to the rises we should suffer anyway from inflationary forces. (See White Paper CMD. 4289 of Feb. 1970).

4. HOW MUCH WOULD THE COST OF LIVING RISE?

Not merely would food prices rise. But a heavy new tax, called the Value-Added Tax, would have to be imposed on virtually all the necessities of life, including many foods. Social Security Contributions imposed on the wage-earner and salary-earner and the employer would also be much higher. Altogether, the cost of living would be pushed up permanently to a level of about 1s. 6d. in the £ above what it would be if we did not join. For old people and large families, the extra burden would probably be at least 2s.–2s. 6d. in the £. This would set wages and prices chasing one another faster than ever before.

5. WHAT EFFECT WOULD JOINING THE COMMON MARKET HAVE ON BRITAIN'S BALANCE OF PAYMENTS?

It would load on to us a staggering, permanent and unnecessary new burden. If Britain is to be strong and speak vigorously in the world's counsels, we must pay our way in the world. Joining the Common Market would make this impossible. The extra burden of higher food prices and "tribute" payments to the Brussels agricultural relief funds, would come to £500m. or £600m. a year. We should lose exports all over the world because of high labour costs, and lost preferences in the Commonwealth and E.F.T.A. Altogether, at least £500m. a year of exports would be lost; and the gain in exports to the Six would be more than cancelled out by a rise in imports from them. The total world market for British industry would be permanently narrowed. *The extra burden on the British balance of payments would be over £1,000m. a year, rising year by year.* This would force any British Government into squeezes, freezes and new borrowings from abroad.

6. WHAT ABOUT WAGES IN THE COMMON MARKET?

In all the Common Market countries except Germany, real wages are lower than in Britain. This is because the cost of living in the Six is so much higher. It is only in Germany that even money wages are appreciably higher than here. The latest figures for a male worker's hourly earnings *in money* in the various countries are as follows.

	s.	d.
Italy	7.	4.
France	8.	4.
Britain	10.	8.
Holland	10.	9.
Belgium	10.	10.
W. Germany	13.	5.

(Sources: official British and E.E.C. statistics: See "Financial Statistics" November 1970 and "Equipment & Productivity Gazette" August 1970). As the cost of living is 10%–20% higher in the Common Market, *it is clear that REAL wages in Britain are much higher than in any Common Market country except Germany.* This is confirmed by the fact that Britain has more cars, T.V. sets and telephones per head than the Common Market. (See "The Common Market and The Common Man" p.21 published by E.E.C. Press and Information).

7. WHO PAYS FOR SOCIAL SERVICES IN THE COMMON MARKET?

Very largely the wage-earners and salary-earners themselves and the poorer families. Here are the weekly social security contributions paid by a wage-earner with £20 a week in Britain and Germany respectively:–

Contribution (£.s.d.)	Employee	Employer
Britain	1.7.10.	1.9.1.
Germany	2.14.0.	3.0.0.

The weekly social security tax on the employee is thus twice as high in Germany as here. In France and Italy the employer's contribution is between £4 and £6 a week. The employer's contribution is largely passed on in higher prices, which makes the cost of living, and export prices, still higher. And none of these countries have a National Health Service, which like ours is largely free.

8. WHO PAYS THE TAXES IN THE COMMON MARKET?

Mainly those least able to bear them, through food taxes and the Value-Added Tax–whereas in Britain and Scandinavia, a much fairer share is paid by those best off. The following is the percentage of total national revenue raised in various countries by direct taxes, which are higher for the rich and lower for the poor, and therefore fall on those best able to pay them:

	%
Sweden	51.3
Denmark	45.8
Britain	37.0
Italy	22.4
France	17.4

(Source: O.E.C.D. Statistics).

These figures largely explain why there is so much visible inequality and poverty in France and Italy, and such powerful Communist Parties, and why Parliamentary Government is unstable. The Common Market is now demanding that all members shall adopt the same tax system.

9. HOW BAD IS TAX EVASION IN THE COMMON MARKET?

Very bad indeed in France and Italy especially. *In France, according to the French National Statistical Institute, about one-third of income-tax revenue due, or between £1,070 millions and £1,380 millions is lost through illegal evasion every year* ("The Times" October 27th, 1970). In Italy, 50% of income-tax revenue is lost through evasion, according to Signor Aristide Mondani, an eminent Italian Professor of Statistics ("Guardian" September 10th, 1970). If Britain were to join the Common Market, the British tax-payer would pay through the nose to relieve wealthy French and Italian tax evaders. In the end, the atmosphere of tax fraud, which corrupts so much of Italian and French society, and is a major cause of political extremism, would tend to infect Britain.

10. WHAT EFFECT HAS THE ROME TREATY HAD ON GROWTH IN THE COMMON MARKET?

Since the Rome Teaty was signed, economic growth in the Common Market has been slower than it was before. In most of the industrial countries of the world outside the Common Market, growth has been *higher* since the Treaty was signed. Therefore, on the factual evidence, the Rome Treaty seems to have done nothing for growth. The figures are as follows. In 1955-60, before the Rome Treaty became effective, annual growth in the Common Market was 5.3%. In 1960-69, after the Treaty had come into force, it had fallen to 5.1%. But in all the Western countries of the O.E.C.D. *apart from the Common Market*, growth more than doubled in the same period. In addition, in all the European O.E.C.D. countries other than the Six, and in all E.F.T.A. countries other than Britain, growth has been much *higher* since 1960 than before.

11. WHAT EFFECT WOULD JOINING THE COMMON MARKET HAVE ON BRITAIN'S ECONOMIC GROWTH?

The resulting balance of payments deficit and squeeze policies would slow down our growth to something like 1% a year at the very best. There could be no relief from this through devaluation, because exchange rates are in future to be rigidly fixed in the Common Market. *If, therefore, we had joined the Common Market in 1960, wages in Britain would be £5 a week lower today than they are.*

12. WHAT ABOUT THE ALLEGED LONG-TERM "DYNAMIC" ADVANTAGES OF JOINING THE SIX?

They are a myth. They do not exist. This has been proved quite conclusively by the thorough, independent report of the National Institute of Economic & Social Research published in its Review for November 1970. This report shows that the *Common Market share of exports to the world outside the Six has fallen steadily since the signing of the Rome Treaty.* It also shows that since that time economic growth has worsened within the Six, and improved in the rest of the O.E.C.D. The Institute's comment is as follows: "It is hard to think that if the dynamic properties of a widening market were really as great as is sometimes suggested, the statistical evidence of their influence would be so completely lacking . . . To accept a heavy burden of 'impact effects' as the price of entry, in the belief that the 'dynamic effects' are likely to be even bigger, would under these circumstances represent a triumph of hope over experience . . . It is hard to see anything which suggest that the U.K. performance would be improved more rapidly inside than outside the Community".

13. WHAT PROPORTION OF BRITISH TRADE IS DONE WITH THE COMMON MARKET?

Only about 20%–both for imports and exports. And there has been little tendency for this share to rise in the last few years. It is less than half of the trade we do with E.F.T.A. and the Commonwealth. The figures for December 1969–November 1970 are as follows:

	British Exports to	Imports from
Commonwealth Preference Area	% 30	% 30.6
EFTA	15.8	15.4
Common Market	21.8	20.0

Since after the Kennedy Round, the Common Market's tariff against British industrial exports averages only about 7½%, the gain from further cuts would be small. Yet this would be the sole advantage from joining the Six. Our trade with the Common Market is increasing anyway without our signing the Treaty of Rome. The figures for "invisible" trade are even more striking. More than 65% of Britain's "invisible" trade is with the Commonwealth and E.F.T.A., and less than 20% with the E.E.C.

14. HOW IMPORTANT IS COMMONWEALTH TRADE TO BRITAIN?

More important than any other section of our trade. Not merely do we sell to, and buy from, the Commonwealth Preference Area about 30% of our exports and imports. *But four countries in the Preference Area*–Australia, New Zealand, Canada and South Africa–*are among our most important and fastest growing export markets in the world.* Australia alone, as was recognised by "The Economist" of August 22nd, 1970, has the potentialities of a second United States. Our exports to Preference Area countries in December 1969–November 1970 were as follows:

Australia	£343m.
New Zealand	£130m.
Canada	£287m.
Southern Ireland	£374m.

Our trade with the Preference Area is now eight times as great in value as in 1938, and twice as great in volume. It has risen rapidly in recent years. Between 1966 and 1969, total British exports to the Preference Area rose from £1,770 millions to £2,217 millions. Our imports from the Preference Area rose from £2,026 millions to £2,530 millions. Our greatest single export market is the United States. Four Preference Area countries come within the next eight.

15. WHAT WOULD BE THE EFFECT ON THE COMMONWEALTH AND E.F.T.A. OF OUR JOINING THE COMMON MARKET?

We should have to erect new, steep and (in the case of agricultural goods) prohibitive tariffs against these countries, who are our traditional and natural trading partners. They have done a large and mutually beneficial trade with us for generations and have built their economies on the expectation that this would last. We should lose as much as they if we shut out their goods. But our action would be so damaging to many of them, that resentment against us instead of friendship would be the inevitable result. Several of the E.F.T.A. countries, notably Sweden, Switzerland and Finland, do not wish to join the Common Market, and deeply regret the British official obsession with it. The same is true of most Commonwealth countries.

The official report of the Commonwealth Parliamentary Association Conference in Canberra in October 1970 says this: "Delegates from Australia, India, Trindad & Tobago, Jersey, Canada, the Isle of Man and St. Vincent spoke on the disastrous effects that Britain's entry into an expanded E.E.C. would have for their economies.

The loss of the British market would threaten the very existence of major sectors of Australia's primary industries. Canadian farmers would also suffer severely if cut off from their traditional markets in the U.K. India too feared that such commodities as tea, jute, tobacco and cotton fabrics exported to Britain from Asia and South East Asian countries would face severe restrictions . . . Countries from the Carribean, dependent upon exports of sugar and bananas to the U.K. market would face financial ruin unless special conditions were negotiated". Millions throughout the Commonwealth are at a loss to understand how Britain could contemplate taking a step which would do as much injury to our best friends in the outside world at it would to our own people.

Published by the Common Market Safeguard Campaign, 55 Park Lane, W.1. and printed by Waterloo Web, 6-10 Valentine Place, S.E.1.

Unit contents

Section 1
Introduction

Contents

Objectives

Having completed the work for this unit you should be able to:

1 Outline the composition and formal powers of the major institutions of the Communities.

2 Describe and illustrate the relationship between the institutions.

3 Describe and evaluate the *formal* decision-making process of the Communities, and assess the importance of the *informal* practices which have developed.

4 Examine the relationships between the Community institutions and the member states (you will be expected to carry this further in Unit 3).

5 Evaluate the roles of the political parties and pressure groups in the Communities.

Study programme

Work for week 2	Source of work	Recommended study time
Essential reading in recommended order		
Introduction to Unit 2	Unit 2, Section 1	10 minutes
The Institutions of the European Communities *Reginald Dale*	Unit 2, Section 2	2 hours
The European Court of Justice *Bryan Gould*	Unit 2, Section 3	2 hours
Policy-making in Practice – the 1965 Crisis *Stephen Holt*	Unit 2, Section 4; Reader, pp. 66–74	20 minutes
The Political Process *David Coombes*	Unit 2, Section 4; Reader, pp. 58–66	20 minutes
Decision-making in the EEC *Michael Niblock*	Unit 2, Section 5	2 hours
Pressure Groups and the European Economic Community *Dusan Sidjanski*	Unit 2, Section 6; Reader, pp. 166–73	30 minutes
Transnational Political Forces *A. Hartley*	Unit 2, Section 6; Reader, pp. 139–43	25 minutes
Conclusion to Unit 2 and self-assessment activities	Unit 2, Section 7	1 hour
Recommended reading		
Choice of articles, see page 90	Reader, Sections 2 and 3	
Reference reading		
The Court of Justice of the Three European Communities *B.A. Wortley, QC*	Supplementary material	

Community Institutions, compiled by *Robert Masterton*	Reader, pp. 53–8	
Broadcasting		
Television Programme 1	BBC 2	25 minutes
Broadcast notes	Supplementary material	20 minutes
Radio Programme 2	BBC VHF radio	20 minutes
Broadcast notes	Supplementary material	20 minutes
Assignments		
CMA P933 41 covers Units 1 and 2	Supplementary material	30 minutes

The unit

This unit is concerned with the major institutions of the Communities. To some the word 'institutions' may sound dull. To others it may sound frightening. It conjures up pictures of vast buildings staffed by faceless bureaucrats, of inflexible and often incomprehensible procedures, rules and regulations. These caricatures hide the real nature of institutions.

What we are concerned with is how power and authority are organized, and in this case how they are organized in the Communities. Who has the right to take decisions? What influences are brought to bear on the decision-makers? Can we play any part directly or indirectly in these processes?

Such questions are difficult to answer in the case of national governments; they become even more difficult in the Communities because of the complex interaction between the institutions of the Communities, and between these institutions and the national governments. To attempt to answer the questions we have to gain not only an understanding of the legal and constitutional framework of the Communities (the formal structure) but also the informal process – the patterns of behaviour which have grown up inside the formal structure which makes the whole machinery work.

Essential reading

The essential readings for this unit are:

1 'The Institutions of the European Communities', by Reginald Dale (Section 2 of this unit).

2 'The European Court of Justice', by Bryan Gould (Section 3 of this unit).

3 'Policy-making in Practice – the 1965 Crisis', by Stephen Holt (Section 4 of this unit and Reader, pp. 66–74).

4 'The Political Process', by David Coombes (Section 4 of this unit and Reader, pp. 58–66).

5 'Decision-making in the EEC', by Michael Niblock (Section 5 of this unit).

6 'Pressure Groups and the European Economic Community', by Dusan Sidjanski (Section 6 of this unit and Reader, pp. 166–73).

7 'Transnational Political Forces', by A. Hartley (Section 6 of this unit and Reader, pp. 139–43).

The seven essential readings for this unit constitute a considerable amount of reading, but those in the Reader are short and relatively easy to read. The essential reading is given in a suggested order for reading, but use your discretion to suit your own interests and time. If you find yourself running short of time concentrate on the reading most suited to your interests. To help you with this a brief summary is given below.

Reginald Dale's article (Section 2 of this unit) is a key article and should be read and studied thoroughly. It outlines the institutions of the Communities and examines the relationships between them.

Bryan Gould, writing about 'The European Court of Justice' (Section 3 of this unit) concentrates on one of the major institutions of the Community. The Court is important both as the guardian of the Community Law and because of the crucial political role it plays in furthering the integration of the Communities.

Stephen Holt, in the Reader, outlines a particular incident in the history of the Communities which points up key questions about the independence and initiatory powers of the Commission, and the relationships between the rights and powers of one member state and the Community as a whole.

David Coombes outlines the major institutional and political innovations of the Communities – *engrenage* – the activity of an 'independent' and 'European' body as mediator/conciliator and initiator of agreement between sovereign states. This article is in the Reader.

The process of *engrenage* is examined further by Michael Niblock who deals in more theoretical terms with the whole of the decision-making process of the Communities. He examines the groups which interact in producing Community policy, and poses the questions which will only be answered as the enlarged Community develops politically (Section 5 of this unit).

The two final papers by Sidjanski and Hartley are both in the Reader. They deal with ways in which 'the people' of the Community participate in and influence the decision-making process which affects their lives.

Recommended reading

There is no set recommended reading for this unit. We advise you to select articles from Sections 2 and 3 of the Reader according to your interests.

Obviously if you are interested in local government you will want to read James Swaffield's 'Local Government – Feeling the Impact of Entry' (Reader, pp. 181–6), while if you are interested in the process of decision-making – the way in which some policies are agreed while others are not – you should read Leon Lindberg and Stuart Scheingold's 'Agriculture and Transport Policies' (Reader, pp. 78–92). The introduction to the sections in the Reader should help you find your way around.

There is another article in Section 4 of the Reader (Fenton Bresler's 'Our European Judges' pp. 211–20) which gives a good introduction to the Court of Justice for non-lawyers.

Reference reading

1 'The Court of Justice of the Three European Communities', by B. A. Wortley, QC (Supplementary material).
2 'Community Institutions', compiled by Robert Masterton (Reader, pp. 53–8).

Wortley's paper will be valuable either to those who have a particular interest in the Court and law, or as a source of reference for a particular legal issue.

Masterton's compilation in the Reader will be useful for quick reference on points to do with the institutions.

Note on language

In this unit you will find references to the 'decision-making process' and 'the policy-making process'. It may be that such terminology is new to you, and a word of explanation is needed.

In studying the way decisions are made, whether by an organization such as the EEC or by an individual, there are at least two clearly distinct approaches.

It is possible to study decision-making from a descriptive, case-history point of view. This approach focuses on the details of a particular proposal, the modifications it undergoes as it is discussed, and the particular complex of reasons for the emergence of the final decision.

On the other hand, it is possible to study decisions in more general terms, focusing on the 'process'. This approach calls for an analysis of the way decisions are made, and who makes them, rather than a study of particular decisions. It looks also at the influences and constraints on decision-makers which are applicable in all cases.

Both of these approaches have their value. The first enables us to understand the reasons for the emergence of a particular policy in a particular way at a particular time. This helps us to come to a more realistic appreciation of the likely limits on the development of that policy.

The second enables us to understand the way all proposals are handled within an organization and the organizational and general political factors which affect the emergence of decisions. They help us to analyse the factors which are likely to influence the development at any particular policy.

The Community plumbing system flow chart illustrating the main relationships between the
Community Institutions and the national governments

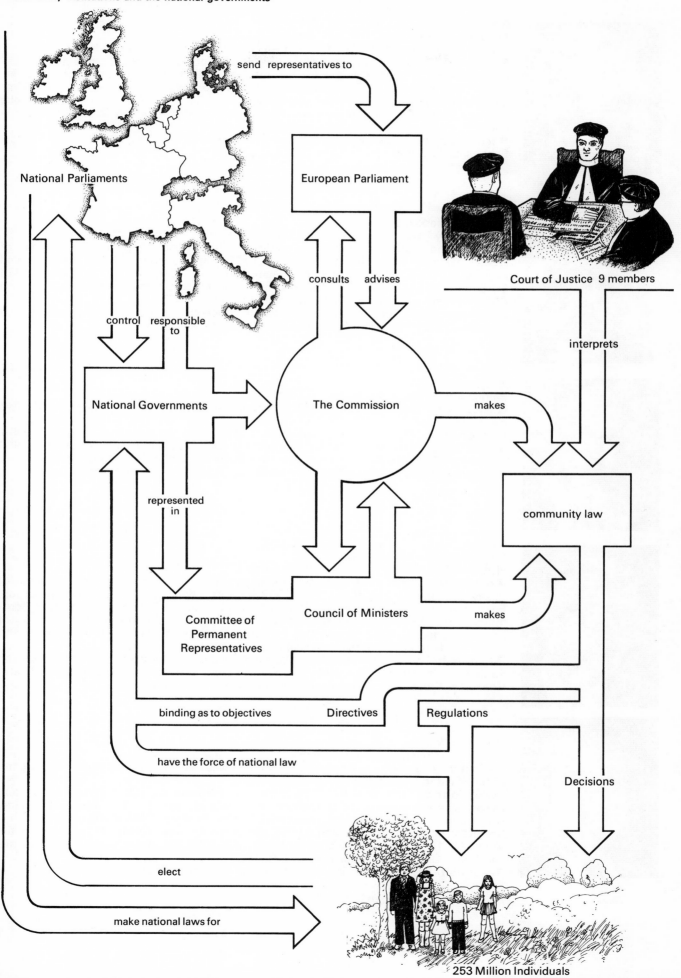

send representatives to

National Parliaments

European Parliament

Court of Justice 9 members

consults   advises

control   responsible to

interprets

National Governments

The Commission

makes

community law

represented in

Committee of Permanent Representatives

Council of Ministers

makes

binding as to objectives   Directives   Regulations

have the force of national law

Decisions

elect

make national laws for

253 Million Individuals

Commission President and Vice-Presidents

Name
François-Xavier Ortoli
Nationality French   **Born** 1925 Ajaccio. Married with four children.
Background Lawyer. Ministry of Finance and Economic Affairs of France. 1958–1962 Commission's Director-General for the Internal Market and Harmonization of Laws. 1962–1966 Private *Cabinet* of M Pompidou. 1966 Head of French Planning Commission. 1968 Elected to French National Assembly. 1967–1972 Minister of Public Works, of Education, of Economy and Finance, and of Industrial and Scientific Development.
Responsibility Commission President. In charge of General Secretariat, Legal Service, Spokesman's Group and Security Office.

Name
Wilhelm Haferkamp
Nationality German   **Born** 1923 Duisburg
Background Cologne University graduate. 1950 Head of Social Department of DGB — German Trade Union Federation. 1962–1967 member of DGB executive and head of Economic Policy Department. Member of ECSC Consultative Committee and of EC Economic and Social Committee. 1958–1966 and 1967 Socialist member of North Rhine-Westphalia Landtag. Became Commissioner in 1967.
Responsibility Commission Vice-President (since 1970). In charge of Economic and Monetary Affairs including ECSC Credit and Investments.

Name
Patrick John Hillery
Nationality Irish   **Born** 1923 Miltown-Malbay, Co Clare. Married with two children.
Background Qualified and practised as a doctor until he went into politics in 1959. Served as Minister of Education, of Industry and Commerce, and of Labour. 1969 Minister of Foreign Affairs — leads Irish delegation in membership negotiations.
Responsibility Commission Vice-President. In charge of Social Policy.

Name
Carlo Scarascia Mugnozza
Nationality Italian   **Born** 1920 Rome
Background Doctor of Law and barrister. 1953 Christian Democrat member of Italian Chamber of Deputies. 1958–1962 Vice-President of CD Parliamentary Group. For ten years he was a member of the Italian Chamber of Deputies Agricultural Committee. 1962–1963 Secretary of State for Education. June-December 1963 Secretary of State for Justice. 1962 Member of European Parliament. March 1972, Member and Vice-President of Commission succeeding M. Mansholt.
Responsibility Commission Vice-President. In charge of relations with the European Parliament in conjunction with the Commission President; Environmental Policy; Consumer Protection; Transport Policy; Press and Information.

Name
Sir Arthur (Christopher) John Soames
Nationality British   **Born** 1920. Married Miss Mary Churchill, youngest daughter of Sir Winston Churchill. Five children.
Background Eton and RMC Sandhurst. Coldstream Guards — served in Western Desert and on intelligence operations in Italy and France. 1946 Assistant Military Attaché in Paris. 1950–1966 Conservative MP for Bedford. 1955 Parliamentary Under-Secretary of State, Air Ministry. 1957 Parliamentary and Financial Secretary to the Admiralty. 1958 Secretary of State for War. 1960–1964 Minister of Agriculture, Fisheries and Food. 1968–1972 Ambassador to France.
Responsibility Commission Vice-President. In charge of External Relations.

(See also pp. 134 and 160)

Section 2
The Institutions of the
European Communities
Reginald Dale

Contents

Reginald Dale has been Common Market Correspondent of the *Financial Times* for the past five years. After leaving Oxford in 1963, he spent four years specializing in European affairs in the *Financial Times* London office, before moving to Brussels in 1968.

Course team introduction

This article is important not only to this unit, but also to the rest of the course.

Reginald Dale summarizes the composition and functions of the major institutions of the Communities – the Commission, the Council of Ministers, the Court of Justice, the European Parliament, and the various specialist advisory committees. He also indicates in outline the formal and informal relations between these bodies in the formulation of policy – the process of decision-making. You should study particularly carefully the sections on the Council of Ministers, the Commission and the European Parliament. A later paper deals specifically with the Court of Justice, so you can read that section in Dale's article quickly.

An appreciation of these relationships and of the process of decision-making is the essential basis for understanding how the EEC functions. If you do not understand the processes outlined in this unit, you may find difficulty in understanding the detailed studies of the emergence of particular policies in later units.

As you read this article look for the following:

1   The composition of each of the major institutions.

2   The formal task which, according to the Treaties, each institution is supposed to perform.

3   The relationship which has developed between the institutions, especially:

   a   The Council/Commission dialogue which produces decisions, and the role of the Committee of Permanent Representatives (Coreper) in this dialogue.

   b   The roles of Parliament, the Court of Justice and the specialized advisory committees in relation to the central decision-making process.

4   Contrast the formal relationships between the institutions laid down by the Treaties with the informal processes which have grown up. Assess the value of such informal links in furthering the purposes of the Communities. (This article introduces these subjects, they will be treated further as the unit proceeds.)

Article 189

In order to carry out their task the Council and the Commission shall, in accordance with the provisions of this Treaty, make regulations, issue directives, take decisions, make recommendations or deliver opinions.

A regulation shall have general application. It shall be binding in its entirety and directly applicable in all member-states.

A directive shall be binding, as to the result to be achieved, upon each member-state to which it is addressed, but shall leave to the national authorities the choice of forms and methods.

A decision shall be binding in its entirety upon those to whom it is addressed.

Recommendations and opinions shall have no binding force.

(Treaty establishing the European Economic Community (Rome, 25 March 1957) Cmnd 4864.)

The Institutions of the European Communities
Reginald Dale

1
Introduction
The European Community's institutions were designed by its 'Founding Fathers' to provide a carefully balanced framework inside which the member states would progressively advance along the road to a European federation. Today, over twenty years since the first Community (the European Coal and Steel Community) was founded, the federal enthusiasm of the 1950s' idealists may easily seem naive, or at least unrealistic. The Community is still largely preoccupied with strictly national interests, in Britain 'federalism' is to many people a concept that must be strenuously resisted, and more and more thinkers and politicians among the original six member countries believe that the way forward must consist of pragmatic and concrete steps rather than a leap of supranational faith.

Over the years, the delicate balance between the institutions has, perhaps predictably, been thrown out of line. The Council of Ministers, the arena in which governments openly promote and defend their national interests, has gained power at the expense of the potentially more supranational bodies, the Commission and the European Parliament (Holt, Unit 2, Section 4). But the Community's decision-making process still basically depends on the interplay between the four main institutions conceived in the 1950s – the Commission, the Council, the Parliament and the Court of Justice. This paper examines the four main institutions in that order, concluding with a brief sketch of some of the many less publicized organs and committees that play an essential role in the daily job of running the Community's affairs.

2
The Commission
The complex working of the Community's institutional machinery is often misunderstood – in the original six member countries as well as in Britain – and the Community is often attacked as being already too centralized. A frequent argument against British membership was that the UK would be submitting the running of its affairs to 'bureaucratic control from Brussels' (Northedge, Unit 1). This is a fear which at first sight would seem to be amply justified by that most maligned of all Community institutions, the Commission. Even the massive Berlaymont building which houses it, in one of the uglier areas of the Belgian capital, gives an impression of technocracy dwarfing ordinary human dimensions. It has been variously dubbed the 'Berlaymort' because of the noxious effects of its ventilation system, and the 'Berlaymonster'.

But the Commission of the European Communities, to give it its proper title, is not an enormous bureaucracy by national standards. With a total staff of 5500 employees, from errand boys to directors general, it must cope with the whole range of Community business from the price of rapeseed to nuclear physics. It has, in fact, since 1967, combined under one roof the executive functions of all three European Communities – the EEC (or Common Market), Euratom, and the European Coal and Steel Community (ECSC) (Section 6). By comparison, one of the larger British Ministries might employ well over 20,000 people to deal with one policy sector alone (Wallace, Unit 3). And even where the Commission's powers are greatest, for instance in enforcing the common policy on free competition, its staff is distinctly thin on the ground: the entire staff of the Commission's competition department is half the size of the German National Cartel Office.

But if the scale is smaller, the hierarchical atmosphere of national civil service organizations is equally pervasive in Brussels. The plush top thirteenth floor, on which the Commissioners (pp. 92, 134 and 160) themselves have their offices, is the only one on which the windows actually open, and at the lower levels there are the familiar

The lair of the Berlaymonster! The Berlaymont Building on the Place Schuman in Brussels is the headquarters of the Commission

arguments over the shape and size of office carpets. The administrative-grade *fonctionnaires* (graded from A1 to A7) are split up into 18 directorates-general, each with the same pyramidical structure of command. The principal exceptions are the spokesman's group of ten members, directly responsible to the President, and the members of the *cabinets*, or personal staffs, of the Commissioners – both of whom regarded themselves as something of an elite. (The spokesman's group is responsible for releasing day-to-day information on the Commission's activities to journalists.)

It is into this structure that British, Irish and Danish civil servants have gradually inserted themselves since the beginning of 1973. The nine members of the old six-country Commission all resigned at the end of 1972, and were replaced by a new 13-strong Commission, to which the 'big' countries (Britain, France, Germany and Italy) each nominated two members, and the others one each. The new President is M. François-Xavier Ortoli, of France (the first time a Frenchman has been President), and Britain's representatives are Sir Christopher Soames and Mr George Thomson (pp. 92 and 160). 6

The new Commissioners brought their own personal staffs, or *cabinets*, with them, but elsewhere in the building a delicate grafting operation was undertaken to make places for the new employees. Over 200 of the original personnel were given golden handshakes to make way for the newcomers, in a re-shuffle which caused some long-standing Eurocrats considerable personal bitterness, and an additional 600 or so new posts have been created, of which 260 are A grade. In the share-out of jobs in Brussels, Britain was particularly keen to make its way up to its unofficial 7 staff quota of 18 per cent by the end of 1973, especially in the higher administrative grades where the key decisions are taken.

For despite the fact that the Commission personnel are meant to renounce any special links with their country of origin and become 'European' once they arrive in Brussels, in practice this is virtually impossible. Nationals of one particular country often cluster together in specific Directorate Generals, and although French is the unofficial working language of the Commission, different linguistic pockets tend to form in the various policy areas. British officials make no secret of the fact that the staff from the UK will be expected to inject 'an intelligent British viewpoint' into the Commission's deliberations (Niblock, Unit 2, paragraph 7). 8

Nevertheless, it is perhaps worth recalling what the Treaty of Rome specifically lays down in this context. According to Article 157, 'the members of the Commission shall perform their duties in the general interest of the Community with complete independence. In the performance of their duties, they shall not seek or accept instructions from any government or other body . . .'. 9

In practice, however, the governments bargain over the key portfolios, and Commissioners often refer back informally to their national capitals to assess the latest state of official thinking. Britain fought hard to acquire the two portfolios it wanted for Sir Christopher Soames and Mr George Thomson – external relations (Twitchett, Unit 4), and regional policy (Holland and Drewer, Unit 8) – and many of the other governments were equally keen to promote what they saw as their own interests when the jobs were distributed. 10

3
The Commission
and the Council

There are plenty of people in Brussels who will maintain that this seemingly illicit form of national interference is not only inevitable, but also often essential to the Community's functioning. The Commission's role under the Treaties is to act as policy initiator, mediator between governments, and watchdog of the Treaty rules. It has often been described as the 'motor' of the Community. But it is pointless, it is argued, for the Commission to make proposals that are clearly unacceptable to one or more of the member states, and the specific interests of each country must be taken into account in the calculation of the interests of all. 11

For whether the Commission likes it or not, there are few fields in the Community in which it has the power of independent action. It can propose policies, and it carries them out once they have been agreed, but it is the Council of Ministers (the official representatives of the national governments) that decides them. The Commission, for example, is responsible for running the Common Agricultural Policy and the Farm Fund (Ritson, Unit 6), but it was the member states that defined the policy. In 1970, the Commission assumed responsibility for trade negotiations with other countries, under the common commercial policy, but it must still be given the authorization of the Council before it opens negotiations and again before it concludes an agreement[1] (Twitchett, Unit 4). 12

It is in the role of Community policeman that the Commission has the most specific powers (Gould, Unit 2, Section 3.1.1). It may take member governments to the Communities' Court of Justice in Luxembourg if they disobey Treaty regulations or Council directives. The number of cases brought by the Commission against states averages around two or three a year, although it rose to eleven in 1969. In that year the actions included a successful case against France for operating an illegal export credit system and an action against Italy for applying allegedly discriminatory taxes on imported wools. 13

[1]Article 113 of the Treaty of Rome gives this responsibility to the Commission at the end of the transitional period.

Directorates General of The Commission

DG I — External relations
DG II — Economic and financial affairs
DG III — Industrial, technological and scientific affairs
Training and Education Group
DG IV — Competition
DG V — Social affairs
DG VI — Agriculture
DG VII — Transport
DG VIII — Development aid
DG IX — Personnel and administration
DG X — Press and Information
DG XI — External trade
DG XII — *
DG XIII — Dissemination of information
DG XIV — Internal market and approximation of legislation
DG XV — *
DG XVI — Regional policy
DG XVII — Energy and Euratom safeguards
DG XVIII — Credit and investments
DG XIX — Budgets
DG XX — Financial control
*Directorates-General abolished as a result of reorganization.

Nine Governments

Interest Groups

appoint

advises

European Parliament

advises questions

Economic and Social Committee

advises

The Commission
(13 members)
and the Directorates General

Executive action

1 after council decisions
2 to implement Treaties
3 to implement European law

Reports violations of the Treaties or of Community Law

represented in consultation, proposals, mediation

decisions

represented in proposals, mediation

Committee of Permanent Representatives

Council of Ministers
Ministers from National Governments

Report violations of the Treaties or of Community Law

Court of Justice

Action

Binding Decisions

Flow chart showing main links between the Commission and the other major Community institutions

In upholding the Treaty's rules of free competition it can fine or prosecute in- 14
dividual companies without reference to national governments, or even necessarily
giving prior warning to the companies themselves (Swann, Unit 5). At the end of
last year (1972), the Commission fined sixteen of Europe's leading sugar refiners
the highest sums ever for allegedly operating a market-sharing cartel. One company
was fined almost £700,000 and the total amount of fines levied ran to over
£4 million. The companies, as is their right, are appealing against the fines to the
European Court of Justice.

But in the framing of new policies, the Commission must rely chiefly on its powers 15
of political persuasion. Most Council decisions are taken on the basis of Commission
proposals, and the member governments usually take account of what the Commission has to say – it is, after all, the only institution that is fully qualified to draw up
common recommendations for all the member states in the areas covered by the
Treaties, and it spends a great deal of its time doing detailed technical studies. (It
may not, of course, venture into fields outside the Treaties, such as foreign policy or
defence, unless specifically invited to do so by the governments.) The Council of
Ministers may amend Commission proposals only by means of a unanimous vote.
They may also reject such proposals.

In specific policy areas, it is in fact often the Commission's proposal, or something 16
resembling it, that is finally adopted. But the Commission has no power to insist
that its recommendations be followed, unless they happen to be backed by an
existing Treaty commitment or a previous Council undertaking.

It is at this level that the Commission's second main role in the Council – that of 17
mediator – comes into play (Niblock, Unit 2, paragraph 26ff). At lengthy Council
sessions, the Commission may in the course of a few hours or days come up with
half-a-dozen consecutive proposals, all of which are progressively abandoned, until
a compromise acceptable to all the interested governments is reached. The final
decision should also, ideally, be palatable to the Commission itself, although this
is not always politically possible. But the Commission must at least try to ensure that
in the horse-trading between member states the overall 'Community interest' is not
completely lost to sight.

If the Commission fails in this task, it may publicly deplore the failure of the Council 18
of Ministers to reach the right conclusion: it may also threaten to resign, as it did in
the summer of 1972 when President Mansholt thought it was not being properly
consulted on the preparation of the Paris Summit conference. But it has never since
1965 sought the open confrontation with governments that President Hallstein
provoked, and lost, over 'supranationality'.[2] Most Commissioners would admit that
this would be risking more than was likely to be gained, and many of them would
also concede that their lives are politically frustrating as a result (Holt, Unit 2,
Section 4).

In this respect, the personalities of the Commissioners themselves are vitally im- 19
portant. While some of his predecessors were more restrained, Dr Mansholt had no
inhibitions about lashing out at the member states, or any other *bêtes noires*, ranging
from General Franco to the British Labour Party. But it can be argued that his
individualistic approach did little to strengthen the 'collegiate' nature of the last
Commission. The political weight of the new Commission will depend very considerably on the way its members interpret their role in the Community decision-making
process. It is already clear that President Ortoli (p. 92), is laying strong emphasis
on the Commission's collegiate character and the Commissioners' joint responsibility

[2]Many who were involved at the time believed that in any event, because of the run of events, a crisis of that
order was inevitable (Ed.).

for decisions. M. Ortoli is much tougher than past Presidents, for instance, in insisting that all Commissioners must be present at the weekly Wednesday meetings, unless they have a really compelling reason to be absent.

The new Commission has not yet had a major confrontation with the Council, and 20 it is still too early in its term of office to draw any firm conclusion about its personal authority. But the British decision to send two such high-ranking political figures as Sir Christopher and Mr Thomson to Brussels was widely regarded as a good omen by people working in the Commission when it was announced in 1972. It is not entirely clear how far their job is seen in Whitehall as being to promote the Commission's independent authority, or whether it is to ensure that British national interests get a fair hearing inside it.

The Commission has its hands full in transforming all the guidelines agreed at the 21 1972 Paris Summit into concrete proposals (Unit 1, Section 5.3). At the same time, its sphere of operations will be extended as new policies on regional, industrial, social and environmental affairs are brought into the Community's orbit. If the past is any guide, it will continue to struggle progressively to increase its powers at the expense of national governments, conscious of the fact that it remains the basic breeding ground of European 'supranationality' and the potential nucleus of a future 'European union', whatever that may turn out to be. Meanwhile, with the new emphasis on the human element in the Community, it will doubtless also be doing all it can to improve its own rather joyless bureaucratic image.

As President of the Commission Dr Sicco Mansholt brought an individualistic approach to the job. 'He had no inhibitions about lashing out at the member states . . .'

4
The Council of
Ministers
But if the Commission is the work-horse of the European institutions, it is the 22 Council of Ministers that provides the Community with its elements of political tension and negotiating brinkmanship. Decision-making in the Community is still largely based on the need to reconcile conflicting national interests, and it is in the framework of the Council that the diplomatic power game between the member states

is most openly played. All the Community's most important decisions are taken by the Council: and it is the Council, as representative of the collective philosophies of the member governments, that most truly reflects the state of European political integration (Niblock, Unit 2, Section 2.3).

The Council is by its very nature a less static institution than the bureaucratically-organized Commission. It has no permanent members – and for the time being, no permanent headquarters. The Ministers have been meeting on the top floor of the Charlemagne building, just across the road from the Commission, while waiting for new Brussels premises to be constructed. The Council's 1000-strong secretariat fills most of the rest of the 14-storey Charlemagne. 23

The member governments can send whatever Minister they like to represent them at a Council meeting, and the Council's composition varies according to the subject matter under discussion. But the Ministers of Foreign Affairs and the Ministers of Agriculture both normally meet once a month or more when Community business is in full swing. The Ministers of Finance are regular participants, and Ministers of Transport, Science or Social Affairs may meet a couple of times a year. The Council of Foreign Ministers is regarded as the senior body, and the Foreign Ministers are sometimes called in to settle disputes when their more specialist colleagues fail to agree. 24

Over the years, the Council has developed its own peculiar working habits and idiosyncrasies. During most months of the year the Ministers are prepared to meet until 5.00 a.m. or later three days running in a marathon session, but would be shocked if anyone suggested they should meet at all between the end of July and the middle of September or over Christmas or Easter. Their calendar tends to become particularly overloaded in December, as they try to meet year end deadlines, and in June and early July, when they work full out to settle outstanding business before the summer holidays. The practice of 'stopping the clock' at midnight until agreement is reached, a feature of the Six's original deadline-packed twelve year 'transitional period', is now a thing of the past. 25

The periods of heavy work also often coincide with the end of each member state's six-month stint in the Council chair, as the President of the moment tries to push through the decisions he has set as an objective for his term of office. The presidency changes hands each January 1 and July 1, passing from country to country in alphabetical order. 26

In January 1973 the Nine started afresh at the beginning of the alphabet, so Belgium was in the chair for the first six months of British membership: the UK, last in alphabetical order, will not have its first turn in the chair until 1977. 27

The presidency does not necessarily bring any particular benefits to the country that holds it – for a small country like Luxembourg, it may mean only a period of intense overwork – although a really skilled politician can use it to his advantage. Perhaps the greatest exponent of the art was General de Gaulle's Foreign Minister, M. Maurice Couve de Murville. But a capable President can often push through decisions and crystallize agreements that might be missed by a less experienced operator. When the going is particularly difficult, the President often finds himself coming under fire, at least in private, from diplomats from other countries. 28

The Committee of Permanent Representatives (Coreper)

4.1 But the pace and efficiency of Council decision-making depends to a much greater degree on the way that ministerial meetings have been prepared in advance, and this is where a much less well-known body, the Committee of Permanent Representatives (often known as the 'Coreper', an abbreviation of its French title) plays an absolutely vital role in the Brussels machinery. The 'Coreper' is composed of the 29

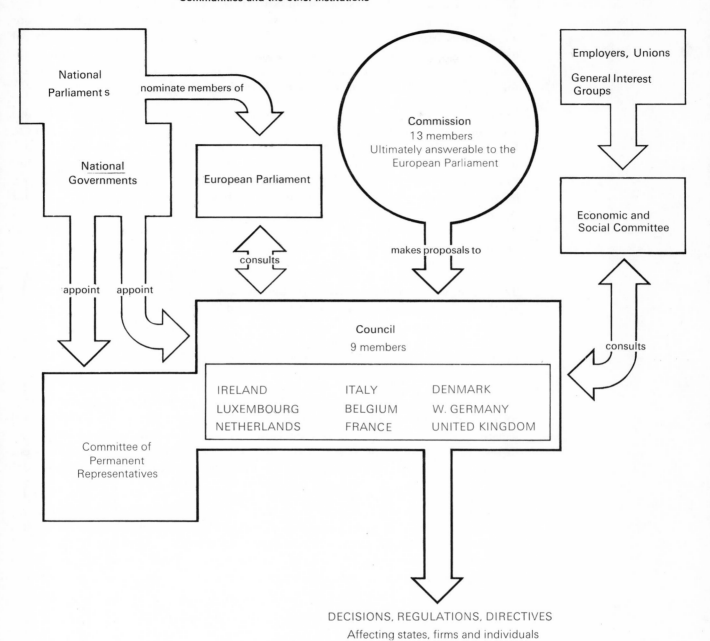

National Parliaments

nominate members of

National Governments

European Parliament

Commission
13 members
Ultimately answerable to the European Parliament

Employers, Unions

General Interest Groups

Economic and Social Committee

consults

appoint   appoint

consults

makes proposals to

Council
9 members

IRELAND	ITALY	DENMARK
LUXEMBOURG	BELGIUM	W. GERMANY
NETHERLANDS	FRANCE	UNITED KINGDOM

Committee of Permanent Representatives

DECISIONS, REGULATIONS, DIRECTIVES
Affecting states, firms and individuals
any of whom may appeal to the court

heads of the member countries' national delegations to the Community in Brussels (Niblock, Unit 2, paragraph 9).

All Commission proposals go first of all to the permanent representatives in Brussels, 30 and are exhaustively discussed by the 'Coreper', or one of its many sub-committees, before reaching a full Council session. The Committee meets at least once a week, usually on Thursdays and Fridays, following the Commission's weekly Wednesday meeting. Sometimes the Committee can reach full agreement on a proposal, in which case it may be adopted by the Council without debate: on other occasions the permanent representatives agree on large sections of a draft text, leaving only a few disputed paragraphs, carefully marked with square brackets, to be settled by Ministers. Where national differences are especially strong, however, the Committee may make little or no progress, and the whole subject is then handed over to the Council.

The Council itself normally meets on Mondays and Tuesdays, sometimes on Thurs- 31
days and Fridays and occasionally on Saturdays, but almost never on Wednesdays
(because that would interfere with the weekly French cabinet meeting in Paris) or
on Sundays. Most of the year it meets in Brussels, but in April, June and October it
meets in greater comfort, in Luxembourg – this was part of the price that Luxembourgers extracted from their partners in return for yielding the High Authority of
the Coal and Steel Community to Brussels in the mid-1960s.

Because each of them has come to defend his own country's viewpoint, the Ministers 32
are usually sensitive to the image they are creating back home when they come to
Brussels or Luxembourg – particularly when the negotiations are difficult or a major
interest is at stake. They will quietly slip out of the Council to give press briefings
just before their own country's newspapers' first edition time (sometimes during a
lengthy session unashamedly using the press to harden their negotiating position for
the next day) and they nearly always give impromptu press conferences and television interviews in the corridors, justifying the position they have taken, at the end
of each meeting.

The whole paraphernalia of the marathon is in fact well designed to suit this purpose. 33
The Ministers on the whole accept that a Community solution must finally be
reached, but they have to convince public opinion, and often their own Cabinets,
that they have defended the national position to the last ditch. A Minister who is out
on a limb may accept at 4 a.m. a decision he would have had to refuse at 10 p.m.
the previous evening – it would not then have looked as if he had fought as hard as
he could to secure a concession.

If they have to give in, Ministers from the Six have so far usually preferred to be seen 34
to have gone down fighting. But situations in fact very rarely occur in the Council
in which Ministers are forced to make concessions without receiving anything at all
in return. The essence of most Council decisions is compromise – the establishment
of at least a lowest common denominator and then the trading off of interests.

There is no question, however, of abandoning a really fundamental national in- 35
terest in this process. The Council, by tacit agreement, hardly ever takes decisions
by majority vote, except on budgetary items, although it is required to do so on a
wide range of issues by the Treaty of Rome. In today's Community, the national
veto is hardly ever explicitly used, but that is because great care is taken to avoid
situations in which one member state might be forced to declare that it was actually
planning to employ the weapon.

It would be too easy to blame this practice on France alone. It is, of course, true 36
that the French have in the past been the loudest exponents of the doctrine of
national interest, and that they successfully boycotted the Community for seven
months in 1965–6, at the end of which the French doctrine of the right of veto on
issues of vital national interest became a more or less established Community practice – although the other countries still officially support the principle of majority
voting. The French also are prepared as a matter of principle to side with any other
country if there is a danger of it being voted down on a vital national interest. But
it is far from certain that the other countries would wholeheartedly support the
introduction of majority voting if the French were suddenly to abandon their opposition (Holt, Unit 2, Section 4).

With Britain, Ireland and Denmark entering the Community, there is perhaps even 37
less prospect of the pattern changing in the coming year. Britain has constantly made
it clear that it approves of the national veto system to which it twice fell a humiliated
victim under General de Gaulle – if only because Mr Heath needs to convince public
opinion that British interests will be just as fully protected as French interests have
been.

In fact, even in the early months of membership it was clear that the UK was ready 38
to play as staunch a nationalistic role as France had done in the past. British Ministers
fought with great tenacity in the haggling that preceded the introduction of the
Common Agricultural Policy in the UK at the beginning of February 1973, and
Britain revealed in the dispute with Luxembourg over the siting of the new European Monetary Fund that it does not mind holding out alone against the rest of the
Community when it feels the need to do so, in true 'Gaullist' fashion. But fears that
the Council would inevitably take half as long again to reach decisions with nine
members than it did with six have so far proved largely unfounded. The three new
members impressed the former six with the brevity of their interventions.

The Council has agreed to introduce some improvements in its working methods 39
in the near future, and the idea of 'Ministers for Europe' in one form or another is
still under discussion. As a start, the Nine might agree to hold their national cabinet
meetings on the same day of the week, so as to free more days for Council sessions.
But there is no sign that the majority of the Nine are yet ready to undertake a wide-
ranging reform of the institutions that would increase the power of the Commission,
or the European Parliament, at the Council's expense. If more power does eventually
accrue to the more supranational institutions in the coming years, it is more likely to
be the result of the hard logic of economic and monetary integration rather than
through any planned or voluntary abandonment of national sovereignty.

5   When European politicians call for a strengthening of the Community's institutions, 40
The European it is, in fact, above all to the Parliament that they are referring. The Council already
Parliament has ample authority to regulate Community affairs according to the whims of
national governments, and the Commission, although occasionally frustrated by its
impotence in some policy areas, has at least reached a kind of *modus vivendi* with the
Council. But the Parliament, and the champions of its cause, have never accepted
the lowly status to which it is condemned by the dominant political forces in the
Community.

The Community's founders clearly intended the status and influence of the Parlia- 41
ment to grow as the Community itself took shape. The Parliament was intended to
provide an evolving element of effective democratic control over the other two main
institutions, and provisions were made in the Rome Treaty, unfortunately perhaps
without setting a deadline, for Europe-wide elections in which voters would directly
choose its members. But apart from a slight increase in the Parliament's control over
a fraction of the Community's budget, due to take effect in 1975, its role has hardly
developed since the Common Market was set up in 1958, and its powers are, on the
whole, no more than strictly consultative. Its only major juridically established
weapon, the right to force the resignation of the Commission, has remained unused
throughout the fifteen years of its existence.

The Parliament normally meets, well away from the other two institutions, in 42
Strasbourg. It is a notoriously difficult place to get to, and in itself no doubt partly
explains the poor attendance and minimal publicity that often characterize its meetings. Its sessions are held in an undistinguished building belonging to the seventeen-
nation Council of Europe (a quite separate institution from the Community), built
as the organization's 'temporary' headquarters in 1949. Work on extending the
'Maison de l'Europe' to cope with the new arrivals from Britain, Ireland and Denmark is currently underway.

The Parliament's secretariat is 200 kilometres away to the north-west in Luxembourg, 43
and the Luxembourgers are constantly on the look-out for ways of persuading the
parliamentarians to hold more of their meetings in the Grand Duchy itself. A brand
new chamber for the Parliament was opened on Luxembourg's Kirchberg in March

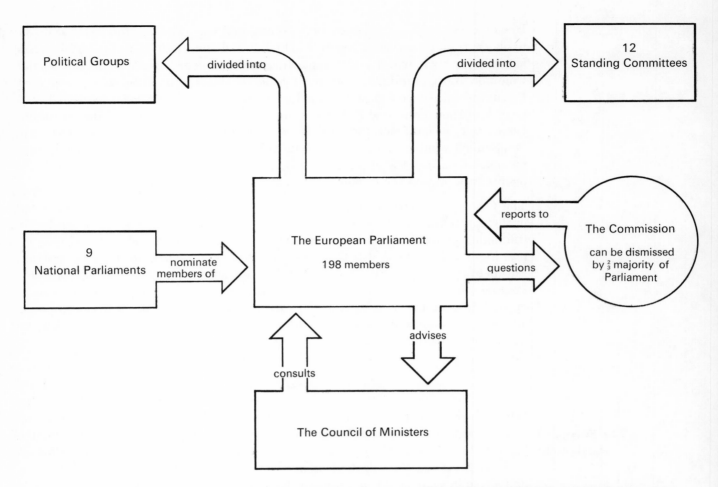

The European Parliament was clearly intended by the Community's founders to provide an evolving element of effective democratic control over the Council and the Commission. However, as this flow chart illustrates, its powers have remained on the whole, no more than strictly consultative

1973, alongside other European institutions; and with the Parliament now meeting as often as once a month, a fair number of the shorter sessions are nowadays held in the Grand Duchy. But there is no question for the time being of a more permanent shift away from Strasbourg. British MPs would in the long run like to see the Parliament moved to Brussels, where, in the UK view, all the Community's institutions ought to be centred in a single 'European capital'. But this, too, is no more than an aspiration for the future.

As it is, the frequency of the Parliamentary sessions, and their distance from most national capitals, makes life doubly difficult for the Parliament's members, who must all be members of their own national parliaments as well. Various suggestions have been put forward in Britain for easing this dual responsibility, but, to begin with at any rate, Britain's representatives in Strasbourg are all Westminster MPs or Peers. Under the present Community system, the European Parliament's members are simply nominated by national parliaments – a process that is said to constitute 'indirect election'.

5.1
Parties The Strasbourg Parliament thus more or less represents the broad political spectrum of political parties in the Community's member countries. Except for the French Gaullists, the deputies do not sit according to nationality but sort themselves into a semi-circle according to political groups, with the left-wing parties on the Speakers' left and so on round to the right-wing on his right. The biggest group is the Christian Democrats, which the Tories have expressed the long-term aim of joining (the Conservatives at present form a separate group) followed by the Socialists and Liberals. The numbers of the groups vary with changes in the balance between parties in the national parliaments, but the size of the groups in March 1973 was as follows:

Christian Democrats, 53; Socialists, 43; Liberals, 25; Conservatives, 20 (18 British and 2 Danish); and the Gaullists, who call themselves the 'Union Democratique Européenne', 19. There are 10 Communists and fellow-travellers, mainly Italian, and the remainder of the 198 seats are taken up by non-affiliated independents, such as the representatives of the Belgian French-speaking federalist group (the FDF-RW) and the Dutch D'66. While the Conservatives sit in a separate group, British Labour Party MPs if and when they arrive in Strasbourg, will sit with the Socialists. The Socialists' group would thus become the largest in the Parliament – unless, of course, the Tories joined the Christian Democrats at the same time.

Even without the British Labour Party, the present Parliament is not 100 per cent 46 representative of national assemblies. The other main missing piece is the French Communist Party, whose members Paris has consistently refused to nominate for Strasbourg (the Italian Communists were admitted as a result of coalition bargaining in Rome in 1969). This is partly of course because the Communists themselves still have an ambivalent attitude to the whole concept of the Community, but it does make life more difficult for the Italian Communist Party representatives. At the time of writing, however, it looked as if a small number of French Communists though not enough to form an official group with the Italians might finally be nominated by the new French Assembly.

In order to be officially classified as groups in Strasbourg, the parties must be able to 47 muster a minimum of fourteen representatives – this qualifies them for various subsidies, so as to operate a small secretariat in Strasbourg, and speaking rights. Because the Italian Communists are not large enough to claim group status, they are officially classified as 'non-affiliated', and the other groups take even less notice of their presence than they otherwise might. But debating in the European Parliament is in any case fairly untypical of most national parliaments.

Because the Parliament has no legislative functions, there is no real interplay 48 between parties in the sense that there is between government and opposition in national parliaments. The various groups have different views, of course, on a wide number of specific issues, but the main effort is devoted towards making the Parliament's collective voice heard by the other institutions (the Commission and the Council), which respectively propose and take the real decisions.

One consequence of this is that Strasbourg debates lack the fire of those, say, at 49 Westminster. Another is that by constantly striving for unanimity, to give their verdict greater weight in Brussels, the deputies often have to water down the terms of more controversial resolutions. Most of the resolutions that are passed in any case lack interest because there is no real political power behind them.

5.2 The Parliament must, according to the Treaties, be consulted on a wide range of 50
Powers Community decisions, and also on Commission proposals (Niblock, Unit 2, Section 4.2). The deputies' views are occasionally listened to, and they can sometimes create a minor stir by putting pertinent written or oral questions to the Commission, but they have no authority to block or modify Community decisions once they have been taken by the Council.

Until recently the principal, and indefatigable questioner of the Commission was 51 Dutch Socialist Henk Vredeling. He has now left the Parliament to become Minister of Defence in the new Hague government, but there is no doubt that his persistent questions, mainly written, helped as a continual reminder to the Commission of its responsibilities to the Parliament – even if they probably had little effect in actually altering major policies. At the same time, the arrival of the Westminster MPs, together with a large contingent of British journalists, has helped to provide more publicity for the Parliamentarians opinions and grievances. Many people in Brussels and Strasbourg, including the British MPs, believe that the attraction of greater

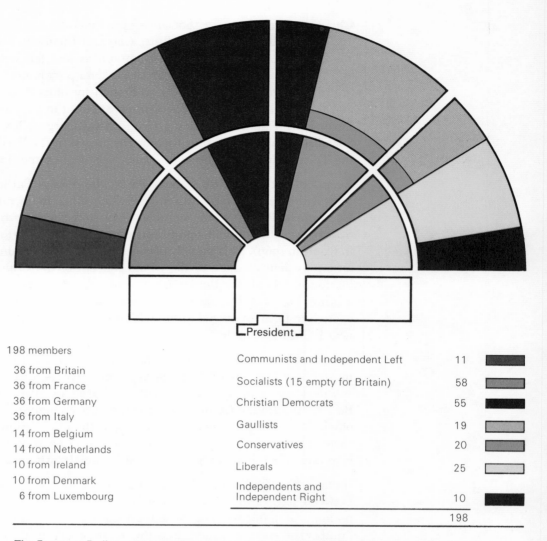

198 members	Communists and Independent Left	11
36 from Britain	Socialists (15 empty for Britain)	58
36 from France	Christian Democrats	55
36 from Germany		
36 from Italy	Gaullists	19
14 from Belgium	Conservatives	20
14 from Netherlands	Liberals	25
10 from Ireland		
10 from Denmark	Independents and	
6 from Luxembourg	Independent Right	10
		198

The European Parliament more or less represents the broad political spectrum of parties in the Community's member countries

publicity will be a key element in increasing the Parliament's authority and giving a wider public airing to European issues.

Equally, the introduction at the beginning of 1973 of a new 'Question Time', 52 largely modelled on Westminster practice, is showing some signs of increasing the degree to which Commissioners have to worry about defending their policies in Strasbourg. Commissioners and Council representatives, are subjected to a series of off-the-cuff oral questions on their policies, which they can sometimes find embarrassing.

The Parliament's most specific weapon is the right to force the resignation of the 53 entire Brussels Commission by the adoption of a motion of censure. (This requires a two-thirds majority of those voting, representing at least half the Parliament's members.) But even this is a largely unsatisfactory privilege – in the first place the Parliament has no say in the reappointment of new Commissioners, and in the second the weapon is basically directed at the wrong enemy. Any serious grievance on the Parliament's part is much more likely to be the fault of the Council, against which it has no formal recourse.

At the time of writing only one motion of censure has been officially tabled in 54 Strasbourg, and that was at the end of 1972 – but the motion was withdrawn before it was put to the vote in December. The motion took the Commission to task for failing to introduce new proposals designed to increase the Parliament's powers of control over the Community budget. The Parliament is already due to gain a slight increase in its budgetary powers in 1975, quite apart from the Commission's new proposals, after which it is meant to have the last word in the small section of the budget devoted to administrative matters. But here again, the power is largely illusory as the size of the budget in practice depends on decisions taken by the Council of Ministers, over which the Parliament has no control.

Nevertheless, the budget is a key issue.[3] The Community is moving towards a 55 system under which the budget will soon be entirely financed by its 'own resources' – that is to say, customs duties and levies on farm imports, as well perhaps as a fraction of VAT receipts, will go directly to the Community rather than passing into national exchequers. Most of the member governments accept that the loss of control over these funds by national parliaments should be compensated by some increase in the powers of the Strasbourg Parliament at Community level. Logically, the same should apply in all other areas where parliaments are losing control over policies to central Community institutions.

For a long time, the argument on increasing the Parliament's powers has gone 56 round in circles – the Parliament cannot be given more powers until it is directly elected, and it cannot be directly elected until it has more power. France has always obstinately opposed any move to organize direct elections in practice, although the French say they agree to the principle – it is, after all, laid down in the Treaty. The British government's view is somewhat similar. The Dutch, Belgians and Italians on the other hand are strong advocates of direct elections, and a draft bill has been tabled in the Dutch Parliament that would set up the machinery for direct elections to take place unilaterally in the Netherlands to appoint the Dutch quota of deputies. The Dutch, however, will probably wait at least until the new nine-nation Parliament has drawn up its own proposals for direct elections (the six-nation Parliament did so, to no avail, as long ago as 1960).

In March 1972, the Vedel Committee, at the Commission's request, put forward 57 detailed proposals for strengthening the Parliament. They accepted that legislative power in the Community should basically remain in the hands of the Council, as foreseen in the Treaties, but suggested that the Parliament should progressively be given what it called the power of 'co-decision' with the Council – that it should have, in effect, a right of veto over Council decisions. In general terms, the suggestion of their Report was that the powers of the Parliament be increased, before the thorny problem of direct elections, to which there are clearly major practical as well as political difficulties, is tackled.

Although the Six, and now the Nine, have so far failed to agree on increasing the 58 Parliament's powers in any meaningful way, there are some signs that modest increases in its powers may be agreed in the not-too-distant future. The Commission has recently produced proposals, on the basis of the Vedel Report, under which the Parliament would increasingly be given the right to hold a 'second reading' if its views on a policy issue were disregarded by the Council of Ministers, and its powers of control over the budget would be stepped up in a number of, mainly technical, ways.

But it is unlikely that the Nine will agree on sweeping reforms at this stage. In the 59 preparations for the October 1972 Paris Summit both France and Germany expressed themselves broadly satisfied with the present institutional balance, and the three

[3]The Budget is analysed in the *Vedel Report* (Report of the Working Party examining the problem of the enlargement of the powers of the European Parliament, *Bulletin of the European Community*, Supplement 4/72). It is evident from that analysis that the Community budget does not have the same functions as a national budget, and some people believe that it is not a key issue, rather, a flag-waving exercise (Ed.).

Henk Vredeling. As a Dutch Socialist MP he persistently questioned the Commission on the whole range of its activities. He is now the Dutch Minister of Defence.

new member countries have all taken the position that they will need experience of the existing institutions before major changes are made. British officials tend to argue that there are plenty of ways the Parliament can make its voice heard more effectively even on the basis of its present powers.

This was also the line taken by the leader of the Conservative delegation, Mr Peter Kirk, in a memorandum on reforming the Parliament's procedures that he tabled at the first nine-nation session in January 1973. Mr Kirk believed that there were many ways the Parliament could increase its authority without changing the existing Treaties, and caused a certain amount of resentment in Strasbourg by telling the older members, in effect, that they had failed to make use of their powers over the past fifteen years. The Conservatives put forward a series of proposals that would involve altering the Parliament's procedures so that they would look distinctly 'Westminsterish'. Even while these proposals were still under study, there was some evidence of a slightly more lively style of debating since the arrival of MPs from the new member countries.

European 'capitals' 6 With its new chamber for the assembly, the Grand Duchy of Luxembourg is making 61 a bid to become a more important Parliamentary centre. The Luxembourgers, who are currently also making a bid for the new Monetary Fund, have never been slow to seize the opportunity of attracting Community institutions – the Grand Duchy has, in fact, firmly established itself over the years as the second capital of the Community.

Brussels, the headquarters of the Commission and the Council of Ministers, is the 62 Community's main decision-making centre; but for three months a year (April, June and October) the Council must meet in Luxembourg and the Grand Duchy has gathered together a large assortment of the Community's other departments and institutions. Its special status is largely due to the tough line taken by the Luxembourg

110

Government when the Six decided to move the High Authority of the European Coal and Steel Community (ECSC) up to Brussels in the mid-1960s.

Luxembourg was the original home of the ECSC, the first European Community, 63 founded in 1952. When the other countries wanted to merge the ECSC's High Authority with the Commission of the other two communities (the EEC and Euratom) in Brussels, the Luxembourgers refused outright to accept the move without adequate compensation. After a hard series of negotiations that lasted over a year the Luxembourgers finally received a triple assurance from their partners: the Grand Duchy would remain a Community political, financial and legal centre.

Today, Luxembourg's role as a political centre is reflected in the meetings of the 64 Council there three months a year; the presence of the European Investment Bank testifies to the Grand Duchy's official status as the financial centre, and, as the home of the Court of Justice, it is also the leading legal centre. Mindful of the past, the Luxembourgers have done all they can to provide a permanent base for the various institutions, and a large site set aside on the Kirchberg, a wooded hill on the outskirts of the capital, for the construction of a series of buildings specifically to house them.

7
The Court of
Justice

The latest edifice to rise on the Kirchberg, at a cost of five million pounds, is a 65 controversial five-storey building made out of slabs of rusting steel. The exterior is due to continue rusting until it becomes completely weatherproof, and the interior is filled with specially commissioned works of modern art. This is the new home of the European Communities' Court of Justice officially inaugurated in January 1973. The building has three ultra-modern courtrooms, and the permanent staff is ultimately expected to rise to around 250 people. (Gould, Unit 2, Section 3.)

If the Commission is the official watchdog of the Communities' Treaties, it is the Court 66 of Justice that is the final arbiter in the event of a dispute. Often, the Commission need only point out to a member government or a Community company that it is infringing Treaty rules, and the matter is more or less speedily put right without recourse to law. But whenever the Commission opens proceedings for infringement, the threat of ultimate recourse to the Court is hovering in the background.

The Commission, of course, is not the only prosecutor. The member states may 67 take the Commission to court if they feel that it has not carried out its job satisfactorily, or that it is itself in breach of Treaty regulations – they have indeed done so on several occasions. In certain circumstances, individuals may take the Communities' institutions to court, and the member states themselves may challenge each other in Luxembourg for failure to observe Treaty obligations.

No other international court may, in fact, rule on a dispute between member states 68 over the Treaties' implementation – the Treaties themselves granted exclusive jurisdiction in the field to the Luxembourg Court. But it is a remarkable fact that so far in the history of the Communities no member state has ever brought a case against another one. The governments prefer to complain privately to the Commission, which may then act. Equally, the seriousness of the member states' political commitment to the Treaties is underlined by the fact that no government has ever refused to accept a Court ruling.

In the old Community, the Court was composed of seven Judges, one from each 69 member state except Italy, which had two. The Judges and other officers of the Court must live in Luxembourg, as the Court is technically in permanent session. With the arrival of Britain, Ireland and Denmark, the number of Judges has gone to nine, including the President who is elected by the members of the Court. (Britain has nominated Lord Mackenzie-Stuart, a Scottish judge.)

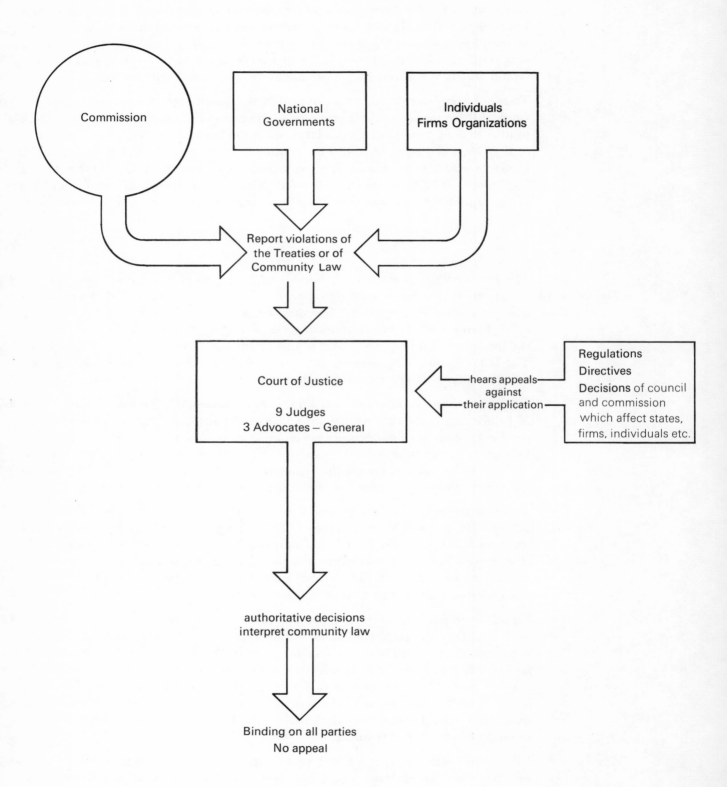

Seven of the Judges must be present to make a quorum in the enlarged Court 70
of Justice.

Nor is there any provision for dissent. The Court's decisions are taken in secret, 71
by a simple majority, and no dissenting or individual opinion is published. The
Judges' deliberations are, in fact, so secret that not even interpreters are admitted and
French is the common language.

The Judges are assisted in their decisions by an Advocate-General to whom there is no 72
real equivalent in British law. The main job of the Advocate-General (of whom there
are four in the nine-nation court) is to give a kind of 'summing-up' together with an
expert legal opinion, in a public session after a case has been heard and before the
Judges take their decision. His role in the proceedings is often crucial.

The number of cases before the Court is constantly on the increase as the Com- 73
munity Law comes to have greater practical impact. In 1971, the Court held 167
public hearings and delivered a total of 60 judgements, based on 18,000 pages of
written procedure. During these cases a total of 72 advocates were heard from the six
member states, not counting representatives of governments and the institutions.
The average length of Court proceedings was eleven months, with the shortest five
months and the longest about a year.

An increasing part of the Court's work nowadays consists in giving preliminary 74
rulings interpreting Community Law in cases referred to it by national courts. Almost
half the decisions made in 1971 were preliminary rulings and the average time length
for these cases was considerably shorter, at around five or six months. The number
of references for a preliminary ruling, the Court says, is 'an index of judicial co-
operation between the Court of Justice and the national courts of the member states,
and of the integration of Community Law into national law'.

Treaty rules governing the reference procedure were intended to promote the 75
penetration of Community Law into national legal systems. Thus national tribunals
may submit any question calling for the interpretation of Community Law to the
Court for a preliminary ruling, if the point is essential for settling a dispute before
them. Reference is obligatory whenever such a question arises before the highest
jurisdiction in a country, against which no judicial appeal is possible.

It is often in this sort of case that the principle of the superiority of Community 76
Law to national law is specifically applied. To take one typical example from 1971:
the German customs refused a Community tariff suspension on frozen beef to a
German meat importer on the ground that 'his past history cast doubt on his
trustworthiness'. The Court ruled that to make the grant of a levy suspension
conditional on 'a subjective appraisal by a national administration' was incompatible with Community regulations.

The greatest number of questions referred to Luxembourg in this way cover the 77
interpretation of the rules of the Common Agricultural Policy, followed by questions
involving social security for migrant workers. But in 1971 there were also cases
involving customs duties, quotas, state monopolies, the common transport policy
and cartels and 'dominant positions'. 1971, according to the Court, was the first
year in which this reference procedure was applied more or less simultaneously by
the courts of all member states. But Community Law was also applied in a large
number of cases by national courts without references to Luxembourg.

The cases that have drawn the most attention recently have been those concerning 78
the Community's rules of free competition. The Commission has been stepping up its
campaign against illegal cartels and market-sharing agreements by imposing heavy
fines, ranging up to several hundred thousands dollars, on individual companies.
It is currently also seeking a ruling from the Court confirming its powers to act against

excessive industrial concentration under Treaty regulations. With the victims frequently appealing to the Court against the Commission's moves, the Court is thus also increasingly playing the role of a court of appeal. In the case of a Commission decision to fine a company, the Court may, on appeal, either confirm, increase, decrease or annul the fine.

The Court's role in enforcing the competition policy can only grow as the Commission itself becomes increasingly active on this front – as it has constantly promised that it will. The Court's basic function will not be altered by the arrival of the new members, although in the longer term court officials are wondering how far the presence of British lawyers will affect its style and its essentially continental traditions. One major difference is that British lawyers can be expected to want to give greater weight to the actual words of the Treaties, whereas the Court up till now has often given general Treaty objective precedence over specific provisions. In the history of the Six, the Court has tended to put the integration of the Common Market before all other considerations. 79

8
Other institutions
and meetings

The Court is the fourth of the main institutions through which the Community takes its most important decisions and charts its future. But there is an enormous number of other more or less institutionalized groupings in which Community business is conducted – ranging from the humblest sub-committee to the periodic meetings of Heads of State or Governments at 'summit' level. 80

8.1
Summit meetings

The summits, such as the one held in Paris in October 1972, are organized when the need is felt to give the Community a new political impetus and to lay down broad political guidelines for a period of several years ahead. The summits are strictly speaking intergovernmental, and outside the Community's formal framework (Unit 1, Section 5.3). 81

8.2
Foreign and Financial
Ministers' meetings

There are two more specific areas where Ministers meet more regularly outside the Common Market framework as such – these are the fields of financial affairs and foreign policy. The Nine's moves to harmonize their foreign policies are co-ordinated by a Political Committee, often known as the 'Davignon Committee' which is composed of senior foreign ministry officials. The Committee takes its unofficial title from Vicomte Etienne Davignon, Political Director at the Belgian Foreign Ministry, and the group's first chairman. 82

Foreign policy co-ordination is not covered by the Rome Treaty and is still therefore conducted on an intergovernmental basis, although the Commission is brought into the discussion when they touch on areas covered by the Treaty, such as Community trade agreements with other countries. The four annual meetings of Foreign Ministers in what is known as the 'Davignon framework' are not therefore official sessions of the Council of Ministers, even though they are presided over by the country that happens to be in the Council chair. The foreign policy discussions are held in all the different member countries in turn. 83

The same applies to the informal meetings of Ministers of Finance, who have been known to gather in Italian Palazzi, Belgian chateaux and German ski-resorts for their quarterly sessions. At these meetings, the Ministers may discuss international monetary developments or matters more directly concerning the Community itself, such as tax harmonization. But the meetings are once again not official Council sessions. 84

8.3
Association Councils and the 113 Committee

Apart from the Council meetings of the Nine there are also regular meetings of Association Councils in which Ministers from member countries meet Ministers from the Community's associated countries in Africa and Southern Europe to discuss the running of the association agreements. 85

The negotiations with non-associated countries are conducted by the Commission, but the member states keep a close watch on developments through their representation on a body called the 113 Committee. The members of this committee, named after Article 113 of the Rome Treaty which set it up, sit in on trade negotiations, but national representatives may not actively intervene in the talks (Twitchett, Unit 4). 86

8.4
The Economic and Social Committee (Ecosoc)

Outside the trade field, the most important consultative committee for general Common Market affairs is the Economic and Social Committee, set up by the Rome Treaty with a permanent headquarters in Brussels. Ecosoc, as it is known, meets around eight times a year for two or three days at a time, and is made up of representatives from three main groups – unions, employers and a so-called 'general interest' group. This last group may contain representatives of the professions, agriculture, trades and crafts, the universities or consumers' organizations. Ecosoc must be consulted by the Council before decisions are taken in certain policy areas, and it is soon to be given the right to express its views on any matter of Community concern without necessarily being asked to. But it has to be recorded that is is only very rarely that the other institutions take much notice of its recommendations in practice. (The British trade unions were boycotting this committee in mid-1973.) 87

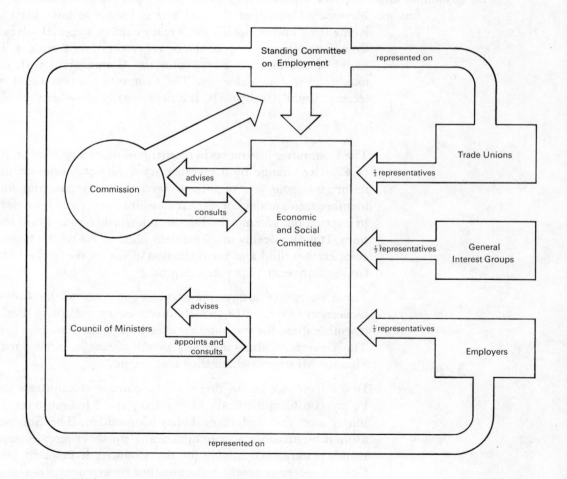

Ecosoc. Although the most important consultative committee for general Community affairs, in practice, the other institutions only rarely take notice of its recommendations

8.5
Consultative
Committee of the
Coal and Steel
Community
A rather more influential body in its specialized field is the Consultative Committee 88 of the European Coal and Steel Community, made up of coal and steel producers, trade unionists and a mixed group of coal and steel users and merchants. This body meets about once a month, and although its views, like those of Ecosoc are not binding on the other institutions, they tend to be taken into account much more often in practice.

8.6
Euratom
Euratom, the nuclear and scientific research community, has two main consultative 89 committees, the first of which is the Scientific and Technical Committee, composed of leading members of the nuclear industries of the member states. This group has to be consulted by the Commission and the Council before certain decisions are taken, in particular those relating to the Community's overall research programme. Probably a more influential body, however, is the General Consultative Committee, which advises the Director-General of the Common Research Centres (CCR) in which the Community programme is actually carried out. This committee, made up of government, research and industry representatives, acts as an important indicator to the Commission of how far the various member governments are likely to accept its proposals on research and nuclear affairs.

8.7
Specialist committees
on economics and
finance
Of all the Community's high-ranking specialist committees, the greatest number 90 are to be found in the field of economics and finance, where there are now no fewer than six separate important policy-planning bodies. The senior of these is the Monetary Committee the only one of the six to have been set up by the Treaty of Rome itself and on which the Treaty confers a special advisory role. The Monetary Committee is made up of senior representatives from the Treasuries and national banks of the member states, plus the Commission, with each country allowed a maximum of four delegates. The Committee meets about once a month, in great secrecy, usually in Brussels, but occasionally elsewhere.

The Committee also meets in moments of monetary crisis or, for example, in the event 91 of a parity change by a member state, and publishes an annual report. Although its original role was mainly to keep the monetary and financial situation of the member states under constant review, it has recently been devoting itself increasingly to international financial affairs and the forthcoming world monetary reform negotiations. It is also deeply involved with plans to create the Community's own monetary co-operation fund and the operation of the 'snake in the tunnel' system of narrower Community exchange rate margins.

These issues are also a major preoccupation of the Community's Central Bank 92 Governors' Committee, which meets every month in Basle when the Governors assemble there for the monthly meetings of the Bank for International Settlements. The Governors also sometimes meet informally during the quarterly meetings of Finance Ministers, which they also attend.

In the economic sector, there are three major committees: the Short-term Economic 93 Policy (or Conjunctural) Committee, the Medium-term Economic Policy Committee and the Budgetary Policy Committee. The Short-term Committee meets around eight times a year and draws up short-term economic projections for the member states and advice for the Council: it helps to prepare the three annual Council meetings at which the member governments co-ordinate their economic and budgetary policies. These meetings are also prepared by the Budgetary Policy Committee, which groups Finance Ministry or Treasury representatives and meets about seven times a year in Brussels. The Budgetary Committee works out preliminary guidelines and follows up with studies of how far they have been carried out in practice.

The Medium-term Committee's main function is to draw up medium-term 94 economic programmes for the Community as a whole, of which the third runs from 1971 to 1975, but it also produces opinions on matters ranging from statistics to employment policies, and takes an interest in Community research and development policies. The sixth of the economic and financial committees is the new High-level Steering Group set up in 1972 with only one representative per member state to ensure maximum secrecy. Its job is to co-ordinate national policies at top expert level in the context of the move to economic and monetary union.

8.8 Other committees proliferate in the agricultural, social, transport, competition and 95
Agriculture, social, tariff sectors. There is a special Agricultural Committee, which prepares Council
transport, competition decisions on farm policy, and 17 Agricultural Management Committees run the
and tariff policy on a day-to-day basis. In the social field, a Standing Committee on Employ-
committees – the ment, grouping Commission representatives, governments (often at ministerial
Social and Farm Funds level), employers and union leaders, meets around twice a year.

At least four times a year there are meetings of the Social Fund Committee, made 96 up of government, employer and union representatives, which gives advice on the policies and operations of the Social Fund and assesses individual claims on its resources. The Social Fund, which is run by the Commission, channels Community finance into the creation of employment and retraining projects.

But its resources are minute compared with the Farm Fund, or European Agricultural 97 Guidance and Guarantee Fund, to give it its full title. The Farm Fund accounts for over 80 per cent of the Community's total £1800 million budget, and the vast part of its resources are used by the Guarantee Section for farm price support. The far smaller Guidance Section is used for measures to improve the structural efficiency of Community agriculture.

8.9 The other main distributor of Community finance is the European Investment Bank, 98
The European set up by the Rome Treaty to promote economic development in the Community's
Investment Bank member and associate countries. Last year the Bank made available loans and
guarantees worth over £200 million. For the 18 African associates and the Community's overseas dependencies, a special financial aid organization, the European Development Fund was set up under the Yaoundé Convention in 1964. This fund has almost £400 million to spend during the five years (1970–5) of the present Convention.

8.10 Two more Community Funds are soon to be set up as a result of agreements reached 99
European Monetary at the Paris Summit. The first is the European Monetary Co-operation Fund, intended
Co-operation Fund to provide the nucleus of a future common central banking system, established on an
and the Regional Fund initially limited scale in April 1973. The other is the European Regional Fund, due
to start operation in 1974 to channel Community finance to regional development projects. Britain hopes to be a major beneficiary of the Regional Fund – its size will to a large extent depend on the success of Britain's negotiating efforts in the Council of Ministers.

**9
Conclusion**

It is on this complex basis of interlocking committees, Ministerial Councils, the 100 Commission and the Court of Justice, that the integration of western Europe has slowly proceeded over the last fifteen years. It is clear that the Community is still far from anything that could properly be described as a federation, but it is equally clear that the underlying structure for a move in a federal direction does exist if the governments wanted to make use of it.

Once the entry of Britain, Ireland and Denmark has been digested, and the reso- 101 lutions of last October's Paris Summit turned into some form of more concrete reality, the next step will be to take another searching look at the way ahead. The target officially set for 1980 at the Paris Summit is 'European Union', a concept that can obviously mean many different things to different people – the reason why it was found possible to agree on the term in Paris!

By 1975, when the next summit is due to be held, the governments will have to 102 start defining in less woolly terms what such a union really means. A great deal of thought will have to be given to the role of the present institutions, their fields of competence, and the relative balance between them. Should, for example as a member of the Commission recently suggested, the European Parliament be the supreme legislative body in a genuine European Union? It seems unlikely that either governments or national parliaments would be ready to accept this in the foreseeable future. What seems certain, however, is that the member states will as far as possible, press ahead within broadly the present well-tried institutional structure. With all its imperfections, it is the only available foundation on which to continue building.

Comments and questions

1 *Work through this section very quickly*. Below are a series of statements about the Communities. Note down whether they are true or false and give the reason for your answer. You may feel that some of the statements are only partially accurate and consequently you would wish to give a qualified answer.

Comments on all these statements, together with references to the text will be found in the Supplementary Material under 'Further comments on Unit 2'.

1 The Communities' policy-making process depends on the interaction of the Commission, the Council, the Parliament and the Court of Justice.

2 The Commission is the supranational executive of the following European organizations:
  EEC
  OECD
  ECSC
  NATO
  Euratom.

3 The Commission is a hierarchical bureaucratic organization split into eighteen Directorates General.

4 Commission staff are expected to represent their own country's viewpoint in the formulation of policy.

5 The Commission may take member governments to Court for disobeying the Treaty regulations.

6 All proposals agreed by the Council of Ministers must be acceptable to the Commission.

7 It is likely that the Commission will increase its powers over policy.

8 The chairmanship of the Council of Ministers changes every six months, passing from country to country in alphabetical order.

9 The Committee of Permanent Representatives has a purely formal role and no real power.

10 Any one member's national interest can be ignored as the Council makes its decision by majority vote.

11 The French support the policy of majority voting and boycotted the Community in 1965 because the other countries would not agree.

12 The European Parliament is directly elected in Europe wide elections.

13 The Parliament has the power to force the resignation of the entire Commission by a unanimous vote of censure.

14 Customs duties, farm import levies and a proportion of VAT receipts will soon go directly to the Community rather than passing through national exchequers. This will give the Community its 'own resources'.

15 The Vedel Committee suggested a reduction in the powers of the European Parliament.

16 The Court of Justice is the final arbiter in disputes within the Communities.

17 Preliminary rulings interpret points of Community Law referred to the Court of Justice by national courts.

18 National law has precedence over the Community Law.

19 The Davignon Committee meets to harmonize monetary policy.

20 The Economic and Social Committee was set up by the Treaty of Rome.

21 The Monetary Committee is the only committee in the field of economics and finance to have been set up by the Treaty of Rome.

22 The Central Bank Governors' Committee meets in a non-member country.

23 The seventeen Agricultural Management Committees run the CAP on a day-to-day basis.

24 The European Agricultural Guidance and Guarantee Fund accounts for over 80 per cent of the Communities budgetary expenditure.

2 This activity is designed to help you make sure that you understand the relationships between the major institutions. Comments on this activity will be found in the Supplementary Material under 'Further comments on Unit 2'.

Community decisions emerge essentially from a dialogue between the Commission and the Council of Ministers. However, other institutions and groups have to be consulted as well – the Parliament, Ecosoc, Coreper, etc. Devise a flow chart which shows the links between these groups in the decision-making process.

Further reading

Roger Broad and Bob Jarrett (1972) *Community Europe Today*, London, Oswald and Wolff.

David Coombes (1972) *The Power of the Purse in the European Communities*, London, PEP/Chatham House.

John Mackintosh (1973) *The Institutions of the Common Market*, Round Table, January 1973.

Richard Mayne (1968) *The Institutions of the European Community*, London, PEP/Chatham House.

Altiero Spinelli (1966) *The Eurocrats*, Baltimore, Johns Hopkins Press.

E. Wall (1969) *Europe – Unification and Law*, Harmondsworth, Penguin.

Section 3
The European Court of Justice
Bryan Gould

Contents

Bryan Gould Fellow and Tutor in Law of Worcester College, Oxford, read law and history in New Zealand before coming to Oxford on a Rhodes Scholarship. After obtaining the degree of BCL, he joined HM Diplomatic Service in 1964 as the top entrant of that year. He spent two years in the Foreign Office, working on European questions, and two years in Brussels, before returning to academic law. He specializes in constitutional, administrative and international law.

Course team introduction

This article deals with one of the major institutions of the European Communities – the European Court of Justice in Luxembourg. It outlines the main features of the Court – its composition, its procedures, and its powers (as laid down in the Treaties of the Communities, and as developed in case law).

Although it is important to understand the role of the Court in furthering the integration of Europe, avoid becoming caught up in too much detail e.g., trying to memorize particular cases or Articles from the Treaty.

The article has been written with the non-lawyer firmly in mind. Nevertheless, the nature of the subject may mean that some people will find difficulty in understanding fully some of the sections. If you do come up against difficulties concentrate on gaining an overall impression of the breadth and scope of the Court's jurisdiction.

Note on Community law-making   *Bryan Gould*

The legally binding acts of the Council and the Commission are of three types.

Regulations are rules of general scope which are directly applicable as law in each member state; they take effect without the need for any action on the part of the legislature or the executive of the member state.

Directives are instructions addressed by the Community to member states which are then bound to give effect to them. The difference between regulations and directives is that the latter require some future legislative action by the member state before they become law in that state.

Decisions are directly binding within the member state and in this respect are like regulations. Unlike regulations, however, they are not rules of general application but bind only those individuals to whom they are addressed.

The Council and the Commission may also make *recommendations* and deliver *opinions* which have no binding force.

A distinction is sometimes made between legislative bodies, which make laws, and executive bodies, which carry them out. But the distinction often breaks down. In this country, for example, a Minister is part of the executive, as the head of his department, but he also has law-making powers, since he may be authorized to make regulations.

The same thing can be seen in the Community. The institutions which make laws, the Commission and the Council, are perhaps better looked upon as executive rather than legislative bodies, since their main function is to carry out the purposes laid down by the three Treaties. Their law-making function is rather like that of one of our Ministers when he makes regulations.

The Commission has wide rule-making powers under the three Treaties, and may also exercise a rule-making power when this is delegated to it by the Council. Thus, for example, many of the regulations made by the Commission concern the Common Agricultural Policy, since the Council delegated to the Commission the task of enforcing the decisions made in that field by the Council.

The Council has an important law-making function, but in general acts only on a proposal made by the Commission. The Commission will formulate proposals, usually after extensive consultations with interested parties, which the Council may then accept, reject, or return to the Commission for reconsideration. The normal rule for voting in the Council is by a simple majority, but when it is exercising a law-making function, a weighted voting system usually operates; this gives greater weight to the views of the larger states and makes it less likely that they can be outvoted.

123

The European Court of Justice
Bryan Gould

1 The Court of Justice was first established in 1952 as the judicial organ of the European Coal and Steel Community, but it has since become an institution common to all three Communities (Dale, Unit 2, paragraph 65 ff.). The three Treaties were modified by a Convention signed in 1958 so as to ensure an identity of texts governing the organization of the Court. Each Treaty is supplemented by a Protocol on the Court, and each Treaty authorizes the Court to make its own rules of procedure, which the Court has done.

2 The powers of the Court vary according to whether it is acting as the Court of one or other of the three Communities. Its powers under the EEC and EAEC (Euratom) Treaties are very similar (the provisions are in many cases identical), but there is sometimes a substantial difference between the provisions of these two Treaties and those of the earlier ECSC Treaty. Where these differences seem relevant, your attention will be drawn to them.

3 Some indication of the Court's role in the Communities is given by the terms of Article 164 of the EEC Treaty which reads:

The Court of Justice shall ensure that in the interpretation and application of this Treaty the law is observed.

This is backed up by the undertaking given by member states, by virtue of Article 219 of the Treaty, not to submit a dispute concerning the interpretation or application of the Treaty to any other method of settlement than those provided by the Treaty. In other words, the Court is given exclusive jurisdiction over such matters.

4 But these bare provisions give very little real idea of the true importance of the Court's role. The Court is in a very real sense the guardian of the three Treaties and the effective watchdog over Community institutions and member states. As we shall see, it is given a very wide range of powers to enable it to fulfil this role.

5 The Court in the enlarged Community is composed of nine judges, appointed for a term of six years, with their terms so staggered that four and five judges are appointed alternately each three years. Retiring judges are eligible for re-appointment. Each member state has one of its nationals as a judge of the Court (the British judge is Lord Mackenzie-Stuart) but while this no doubt reflects some form of informal agreement between member states there is no provision for national representation in the Treaties. Indeed, it should be stressed that the judges are not there to represent national interests but are to act as independent judicial officers. They are protected from pressure from national governments by the secrecy of their deliberations and by the fact that they can be removed from office only by the unanimous vote of their colleagues that they can no longer carry out their functions.

6 The judges must be lawyers and must not hold any political or administrative office or engage in any paid or unpaid occupation. They must live in Luxembourg, where the Court has its seat, and they are entitled to immunity from legal process during their term of office.

7 The judges elect from their own number a President of the Court. He holds office for three years and may be re-elected.

8 In addition to the judges, there are four Advocates-General who are also nominated by member states. They have a status equal to that of the judges and their function is to make reasoned summaries, at the conclusion of the argument before the Court, with complete impartiality and independence. One Advocate-General sits in each case. There is no equivalent in English courts to this officer who is clearly drawn from the French model of a *Commissaire du gouvernement* in the *Conseil d'Etat*. He will

The home of the European Court of Justice on Luxembourg's Kirchberg

often see his duty as including the advancement of a true 'Community view' of the issues. The Court is of course not bound by the views of the Advocate-General, although great attention will be paid to his arguments which are often expressed at greater length than the judgement of the Court.

The Court is organized into two chambers of three or five judges each of whom may deal with preliminary issues (such as applications for legal aid) and hear cases, though actions brought by member states or Community institutions, and references made to the Court from national courts, must be heard by the full Court.

9

Alexander John Mackenzie-Stuart the British Judge on the Court of Justice, being sworn in before the Court

2
Procedure
The procedure followed by the Court owes much to French practice of the *Conseil* 10 *d'Etat* and is quite different from the proceedings of an English court. The procedure is partly written and partly oral. A case starts with the filing of a written complaint; an answer must then be filed within one month, and each party is then allowed to make a second written pleading, usually within a further two months. The pleadings will include matters of fact and law.

The Court will then begin its own investigation of the issues, by taking depositions, 11 interrogating witnesses, asking for expert opinions and listening to oral arguments from counsel for the parties. When the arguments have concluded, the Advocate-General will summarize the issues and recommend a decision. There is no jury. The hearing has up till this point been held in public.

The Court then retires to deliberate in secret. Each judge has one vote (the 12 President has no casting vote) and for this reason there must always be an odd number of judges sitting; the quorum for the full Court is seven judges. When a majority view is reached, the single judgement of the Court will be read out in open court in the presence of the parties. This usually happens some two to three months after the hearing was completed.

The collegiate nature of the Court is both a strength and a weakness. The unanimity 13 of view presented by the Court no doubt gives great weight to its judgements, but the need to compromise in order to produce a single conclusion may sometimes blunt the edge of what may otherwise be a very important pronouncement on Community Law.

Proceedings are conducted in one of the official languages of the Communities, the 14 choice being made by the plaintiff, although there is the major exception that where a member state or one of its nationals is a defendant the language of that state will be used. There is some flexibility however in that the Court may hear different parts of the proceedings in different languages, and witnesses may be allowed to give evidence in their own language.

Costs are awarded by judgement of the Court. Unusually for a court of this 15 character, the Rules of Procedure provide for free legal aid in the case of parties unable to meet part or the whole of the costs of an action. An application for legal aid is made to the Court and need not be made by a legal representative.[1]

There is no appeal against a decision of the Court although there is provision for 16 the re-opening of a case if some important new element comes to light.

3
Jurisdiction
The Court, in the fulfilment of its role as the custodian of Community Law, has an 17 extraordinarily wide range of functions, probably wider than that of any other comparable court. It can, for example, act as an international court, deciding disputes between states; or as a court of review, deciding on the powers of Community institutions and the legality of their actions; or as an administrative tribunal, deciding questions about the conditions of employment of Community servants. Perhaps its most important function from the viewpoint of the development of Community Law is the giving of decisions on matters of Community Law which are referred to it by national courts. Let us look at these different functions in more detail.

---

[1]In the case of a reference to the Court from a national court under Article 177, legal aid will be decided upon the basis of relevant national rules.

3.1
Actions against
member states
3.1.1
Brought by the
Commission

Article 169 of the EEC Treaty[2] provides that if the Commission considers that a   18
member state has failed to fulfil its obligations under the Treaty, it shall issue a
reasoned statement to that effect and give the state concerned an opportunity to
comment within a specified period. If the state concerned does not comply with the
Commission's statement within the time specified, the Commission may refer the
matter to the Court. The Court has no power to initiate proceedings itself. Member
states are bound, under Article 171, to take measures to implement any judgement
of the Court on an issue raised before it by the Commission.

Article 88 of the ECSC Treaty is different and more detailed. In cases where the   19
state refuses to comply with the reasoned statement, it is the state which institutes
proceedings rather than the High Authority (now the Commission). If it does not
bring an action, or its action is dismissed by the Court, it may be subjected to
various sanctions by the High Authority acting with the assent of a two-thirds
majority of the Council. If these measures prove ineffective, the High Authority may
refer the matter to the Council.

A recent example of the cases brought under Article 169 of the EEC Treaty is an   20
action brought by the Commission against Italy in 1970, the complaint relating to
an alleged failure by Italy to make a sufficiently speedy payment of export rebates.
The Court, agreeing with the conclusions reached by the Advocate-General, held
that Article 169 could properly be invoked in the case of an omission or failure to act,
but that the Commission had failed to prove with sufficient precision the extent of
the delay of which they complained.

3.1.2
Brought by other
member states

Article 170 of the EEC Treaty allows one member state to bring before the Court the   21
question of another member state's failure to fulfil a treaty obligation. Before it can do
this however, it must first raise the matter with the Commission which shall, after each
state has had an opportunity to submit its case and its observations on the opposing
case, deliver a reasoned opinion. If the Commission does not do this within three
months of the date when the matter was raised before it, the matter may nevertheless
be taken to the Court, though it is clear that reference to the Court is intended to be
a solution of last resort. There are identical provisions in the EAEC Treaty.

Member states may by special agreement submit to the Court a dispute between   22
them relating to a treaty provision; each of the three Treaties provides for this. Article
225 of the EEC Treaty also allows the Commission or a member state to by-pass the
procedures provided by Articles 169 and 170 and go directly to the Court where it is
alleged that another member state is improperly pleading state security as an excuse
for failing to fulfil its obligations.

No case has yet been brought by one member state against another. This is undoub-   23
tedly because states prefer to settle their differences by negotiation rather than by
litigation.

3.1.3
Brought by individuals

There is no provision in the Treaties for actions brought by individuals against   24
member states. An individual who wishes to sue his government will bring an action
in the national courts; if an issue of Community Law is involved, the national court
may, and in some cases must, refer the matter to the Court (see section 3.5).

3.2
Actions against
Community institutions

The Court is empowered to act as a court of review to ensure that Community   25
institutions exercise their powers properly. Each of the Treaties provides for this
jurisdiction, although Article 33 of the ECSC Treaty is different in some respects
from the equivalent provisions in the other Treaties.

---

[2]Article 141 of the EAEC Treaty is written in identical terms.

3.2.1

What Acts can be reviewed

Article 173 of the EEC Treaty provides that the legality of acts, as opposed to recommendations and opinions, of both the Council and the Commission may be reviewed; Article 146 of the EAEC Treaty is in the same terms. The term 'acts' is nowhere defined; but as it is used in contradistinction to 'recommendations and opinions' we may turn for assistance to Article 189. Here, the terms 'regulation', 'directive' and 'decision' are defined as actions of Community institutions which are legally binding in varying ways, whereas 'recommendation' and 'opinion' are defined as recommendatory only. The clear inference is therefore that the 'acts' which are reviewable for illegality under Article 173 are those which are legally binding, i.e. regulations, directives and decisions (see p. 123).   26

Article 33(1) of the ECSC Treaty is written in different terms on this point, but this simply reflects the different terminology which is used in the Treaty to denote those actions which are legally binding in various ways and those which are not.   27

The importance of the distinction between actions which are legally binding and those which are not can be seen in a number of cases. In *Usines à Tubes de la Sarre* v. *High Authority*, the plaintiffs wished to challenge an opinion of the High Authority. The Court decided that while it was possible that what was called an opinion was really a disguised decision, and therefore open to review, the opinion in question imposed no legal obligation on the plaintiffs and was therefore not reviewable.   28

In *Re Noordwijks Cement Accord*, by contrast, the Commission's argument that their action in removing an undertaking from an exempted category, and thus laying them open to a fine, was not reviewable because it was merely an opinion, was rejected by the Court. It was to be regarded as a decision, and therefore open to review, because it changed the legal position of the undertaking.   29

Each Treaty establishes the same grounds for the review of acts of Community institutions. These are described as follows.   30

a Lack of competence: this is in some ways the counterpart of the concept of *ultra vires* in English administrative law, and is the ground relied on when the Community institution claims the power to do something which it is not authorized to do.   31

b Infringement of an essential procedural requirement: a Community institution may be doing something which it is authorized to do, but failing to comply with some procedural rule. An example of this is the Nold case, where one of the grounds of challenge to a decision of the High Authority was its failure to give reasons for the decision. Article 15 of the ECSC Treaty imposes a duty on the Authority to give reasons for its decisions and the Court agreed that its failure to do so was an infringement of an essential procedural requirement which, if not enforced, would make it hard for the Court to exercise proper legal control over Community institutions.   32

c Infringement of a provision of the Treaty: such an infringement will often involve either lack of competence (since each institution's powers are derived from the appropriate Treaty) or an infringement of an essential procedural requirement, as the Nold case shows. An infringement of any rule of law relating to the application of the Treaty also qualifies as a ground of review under this head.   33

d Misuse of powers (*détournement de pouvoir*): this occurs where a Community institution acts within its powers, adheres to the Treaty and complies with procedural requirements, but uses its powers for an improper purpose. In other words, the inquiry under this head will usually be into motive and objective. An example of this is a case in which the French government challenged certain decisions of the High Authority. One of the grounds of challenge was that the High Authority had introduced these decisions because earlier decisions in the same field had been   34 repeatedly violated. The French argued that the proper action in such a situation was to fine offenders and enforce the earlier decisions, rather than to condone the violations by changing the rules to accommodate them. The Court rejected the argument that the High Authority had misused its powers, holding that it was entitled to take into account the defects of the former system, and in making the new decisions was properly concerned to promote the Treaty objective of prohibiting unfair competition.[3]

3.2.2
Grounds of review

These grounds of review, and particularly the last, owe much to French administrative law. To an English lawyer, they seem hard to distinguish, since they can all seem different aspects of the general doctrine of *ultra vires*. On the other hand, the general scope of these grounds of review, which would have seemed far wider than review in English law fifteen years ago, now seems less revolutionary to an English lawyer who has seen his own administrative law develop similar concepts in recent years (Mitchell, Unit 3, Section 3). **35**

3.2.3
Who can sue

Member states, and both the Council and Commission, may institute proceedings under these provisions. Member states have often availed themselves of this procedure, which must be instituted within two months[4] of the measure complained of being published, or of their being notified or becoming aware of it. In a case in 1971, the Commission challenged the Council's power to negotiate with non-member states over the European Road Transport Agreement, and the Court had to assess the respective powers of both institutions in the matter. **36**

Neither member states nor the two Community institutions need show any special interest in the measure they wish to challenge. For individuals however the position is more complicated. **37**

Article 33(2) of the ECSC Treaty allows undertakings to challenge decisions or recommendations concerning them which are individual in character. In the case of general decisions or recommendations however, undertakings may challenge them only when they involve a misuse of powers affecting them, i.e. only the fourth ground of review is available in these circumstances. The Court has sometimes had difficulty in distinguishing individual from general decisions, but has generally taken a fairly liberal view of the sort of interest an applicant must show in order to meet the requirement that an individual decision must concern him. **38**

Under the other two Treaties, any natural or legal person (i.e. any individual or company) may challenge an act of a Community institution on any of the grounds specified. He must show however that the act challenged is either a decision (as opposed to a regulation or directive) addressed to him, or is a decision which, although in the form of a regulation or a decision addressed to another person, is of direct and individual concern to him. **39**

The Court has been much stricter in interpreting this provision than it has been in dealing with the earlier provision in the ECSC Treaty. The effect of the many decisions on this point is that the Court requires an individual to show that the decision he complains of either was or ought to have been directed to him personally. It will not be enough to show that the decision specially or peculiarly affects the plaintiff. For example, in the Watenstedt Sugar case the plaintiffs contended that a provision which affected a precise number of identifiable persons was not a regulation, but a decision which could be attacked under Article 173(2). The Court held however that a provision framed so as to apply to a class defined in general and objective terms was a regulation and could not be so attacked. This seems a very restrictive view of the circumstances in which an individual can make his complaint. **40**

[3]This was one of the earliest judgements from the Court, No. 1/54 *France* v. *High Authority*.
[4]One month in the case of the ECSC Treaty.

3.2.4
Consequences of annulment
If an action brought under these provisions is successful, the Court declares the act challenged to be void, i.e. to have no legal effect. Where it is a regulation which is successfully attacked however, the Court may declare that some parts of the regulation are to remain in force. Where an act is declared void, the institution concerned must take the necessary action to comply with the Court's judgement. 41

3.2.5
Action for failure to act
Article 175 of the EEC Treaty allows member states or Community institutions to bring before the Court the question of a failure by an institution to act in accordance with the Treaty. There are similar provisions in the other Treaties. An individual may similarly complain if an institution has failed to address any act to him. In either case, the institution concerned must first be called upon to act, and only if it does not 'define its position' within two months of being called upon will the action proceed. 42

3.2.6
Illegality
Even if the time limit specified in Article 173 has expired, any party may, in any proceedings before the Court in which a regulation of the Council or Commission is in issue, argue that the regulation is inapplicable on any of the four grounds specified in Article 173. The plaintiffs in *Meroni S.p.A.* v. *High Authority* relied on the equivalent provision in the ECSC Treaty in order to challenge a general decision (regulation) on which the individual decision affecting them was based, despite the fact that the time limit had expired. The Court upheld their right to do this, but made it clear that a successful argument against the general decision would mean only its non-applicability rather than its annulment. 43

3.3
Actions against individuals
There is no provision in the Treaties for member states, Community institutions or individuals to bring proceedings in the Court against individuals. This is not so surprising an omission as it might seem. Community acts are given legal effect unless successfully challenged, and the onus is therefore on the individual, if he wishes to escape the legal consequences of such acts, to bring the issue before the Court himself. Community laws are of course enforced against individuals in their national courts. 44

3.4
Plenary jurisdiction
The Court is given a number of powers which are less closely connected with the interpretation of the Treaties and Community Law than those so far discussed, but are more like those one would expect to find exercised by any court. 45

For example, the Court has power to award compensation for damage caused by the Community's institutions or servants. Comparatively few cases of this sort have been brought. One such was the Kampffmeyer case, in which German grain dealers sought damages for the loss they had suffered as a result of the Commission's invalid attempt to impose a levy on German importers of French grain. The Court upheld their argument and awarded damages to those who had been affected by the invalid action. 46

The Court may also hear appeals against penalties imposed in accordance with Community laws. Only a handful of cases of this type have been heard. The Court also has jurisdiction over any dispute between the Community and its servants as to the conditions of employment. 47

3.5
Preliminary rulings
Article 177 of the EEC Treaty empowers the Court to give preliminary rulings concerning the interpretation of the Treaty, the validity and interpretation of the acts of Community institutions, and the interpretation of the statutes of any body set up by the Council, where those statutes so provide. 48

The court of a member state may, if it considers a decision on any such question 49
to be essential to enable it to render judgement, ask the Court for a ruling. Where
the court concerned is one from which there is no appeal under national law,
Article 177 provides that it *must* make the reference to the Court. In Britain, this
provision would normally be thought to apply to the House of Lords, the highest
court in the land, but there is an argument to the effect that since there is often no
automatic right of appeal from the Court of Appeal, this latter court would be the
appropriate one to make the reference. It could also act as a sort of filter to make
sure that references are made only in appropriate cases.

The implications of Article 177 (there is a similar provision in the EAEC Treaty) 50
will be fully considered by Professor Mitchell (Mitchell, Unit 3, Section 4). There is
no doubt that this is the most important provision in the Treaty as far as the development of a body of Community Law is concerned. Not only is the Court given the
opportunity of ensuring a reasonable degree of consistency as between national courts
in their interpretation of Treaty matters; but more importantly, it has been able to
assert its own view as to the inter-relationship between Community and national
law.

The Court of Justice in session

The Court has developed a number of principles which it has applied consistently 51
in such matters. In deciding questions of Community Law, the Court leaves to the
national court the application of that law to the facts of the case. But the Court has
gone a good deal further than this, and has pronounced on the difficult question
of the relationship of Community Law to national law. The best way to illustrate this
is to take one of the most important cases which the Court has decided, that of *Costa*
v. *E.N.E.L.* An Italian citizen was sued for non-payment of his electricity bill, and
he argued before the Italian magistrate that he did not have to pay, since the
nationalization of the Italian electricity industry was incompatible with certain
provisions of the EEC Treaty. The magistrate referred the question of the interpretation of the Community Law to the Court.

In the meantime, an appeal on the case was taken to the Italian Constitutional 52
Court who said that the EEC Treaty was only part of Italian law by virtue of an
enabling Act of the Italian Parliament, and that such an Act, like any other law,

L. I. H. E.
THE MARKLAND LIBRARY
STAND PARK RD., LIVERPOOL, L16 9JD

was subject to implied repeal where a subsequent law of the Italian Parliament was inconsistent with it; the nationalization law therefore prevailed and the EEC Treaty was to that extent irrelevant.

The European Court however took a different view. They decided that the EEC 53 Treaty created its own legal order which is directly applicable both to member states and their nationals by virtue of the partial transfer of sovereignty from member states to the Community. Community Law therefore need not defer to an inconsistent national law.

It may safely be assumed that an English court, if left to itself, would, at least in the 54 short term, take a similar view to that of the Italian Constitutional Court. The reasoning would be as follows. The EEC Treaty is part of English law only by virtue of the European Communities Act 1972. That Act is no different from any other Act of the British Parliament, and like all Acts, is subject to implied repeal by a later and inconsistent expression of Parliament's will. In other words, although it is clear that the Parliament of 1972 intended to make Community Law directly applicable in this country, they could not guarantee to do this permanently, since each Parliament is sovereign and cannot be bound by its predecessors. (Mitchell, Unit 3, Section 6, especially 6.6).

The European Court, as the Costa case shows, would certainly take a different view, 55 if the matter were referred in accordance with Article 177. But since the obligation to refer itself depends on the European Communities Act, the reasoning outlined above could remain untouched by any view that the Court might have.

It might be argued that English judges would recognize that which the European 56 Court asserts, that Community Law constitutes a new legal order which is quite independent of national law. Indeed, there is no reason why, after a period of time, our judges should not accept that there has been a fundamental constitutional and political change, which renders the old doctrines of parliamentary sovereignty obsolete. But then the argument becomes one of political persuasion and of prediction of what the judges might or might not do. The question then is no longer the legal question, are our courts *obliged* to accept the 'new legal order'?

4 It will be clear from this brief study of the very wide jurisdiction exercised by the 57
A recent case Court that there is no such thing as a typical case. But it may nevertheless be useful to follow through a recent case of a type which often arises before the Court. In the Internationale Handelsgesellschaft case, a German firm obtained an export licence for 20,000 tonnes of maize groats, and, in accordance with Community regulations, it deposited a large sum of money as a guarantee that the goods would be exported. In fact, just over half only of the maize groats were exported within the prescribed time limit, and the firm therefore forfeited a substantial part of the deposit. They sued for the recovery of this sum in a German court which decided to refer to the European Court certain questions concerning the legality of the Community regulations governing the forfeiture of deposits.

The firm were represented before the Court by a German barrister, and the Dutch 58 and German governments, and the Commission, were also represented. Three other cases involving similar issues were heard at the same time. After the argument had been heard, the Advocate-General made lengthy submissions, which take up twenty-one pages in the Law Reports, to the effect that the regulations in question were perfectly valid. The Court, whose judgement is much shorter than the submissions, agreed. They held in a single judgement that a Community Law whose object was the attainment of a legitimate Community objective could not be challenged as invalid merely on the ground that it strikes at principles enshrined in the constitution of a member state. This would be true, the Court said, even if the Community Law infringed the human rights provisions of such a constitution. This was indeed a striking affirmation of the Court's well-established doctrine that Community Law is a new legal order whose validity and effect cannot be judged by recourse to the rules and concepts of national legal systems.

The story does not end there however. The German Court which had referred the question was not prepared to accept the European Court's assertion that provisions of the German constitution could be overridden in this way, and the whole question has now gone on appeal to the Federal Constitutional Court. The case is therefore a fascinating example of the difficulties which national courts encounter in trying to accommodate the 'new legal order' and the eventual outcome will be of great interest to our own courts. 59

Comments and questions

Having studied this article you should be able to answer the questions below (refer to the text if necessary). Comments on these questions will be found in the Supplementary Material under 'Further comments on Unit 2'.

3 Write down the categories of actions by the Council and Commission which the Court regards as legally binding and those which it does not, and explain the differences between them.

4 Gould outlines four grounds for the Court to review acts of the Community institutions. Note these down.

5 On the basis of your understanding of Gould's paper outline three ways in which decisions of the Court of Justice further the integration of the European Communities.

Further reading

G. Bebr (1962) *Judicial Control of the European Communities*, London, Stevens.

P. Mathijesen (1972) *A Guide to European Community Law*, London, Stevens.

D. Valentine (1965) *The Court of Justice of the European Communities* (2 vols), London, Stevens.

G. Wall (1966) *The Court of Justice of the European Communities*, London, Butterworth.

Bibliography *Where to find your Community Law*, London, British Institute of International and Comparative Law.

Some Members of the Commission

Name
Albert Borschette
Nationality Luxembourg **Born** 1920 Diebirch
Background Studied at Aix-en-Provence, Munich, Erlangen and Paris. 1945–1947 Luxembourg Government spokesman. 1947–1950 Luxembourg representative with French forces in Germany and later with Allied Control Commission in Berlin. Held diplomatic posts in Bonn and Brussels 1950–1958. 1953–1958 Represents Luxembourg on inter-governmental committee which drafts EEC and Euratom Treaties. 1958–1970 Permanent Representative of Luxembourg to the European Community. 1961–1963 Deputy Foreign Minister during enlargement negotiations with Britain. Member of Commission since 1970.
Responsibility Commission Member. In charge of Competition Policy, and Personnel and Administration.

Name
Claude Cheysson
Nationality French **Born** 1920
Background Joined French foreign service 1948. Chief of liaison service with Federal German Authorities, Bonn, 1949. Counsellor to President of Vietnamese Government, 1952. *Chef de Cabinet* to M. P. Mendes-France 1954–1955. First Secretary at French Embassy, London, 1956. Secretary General of Commission for technical co-operation in Africa, 1957–1962. Director-General of the technical organization for the evaluation of the underground riches of the Sahara, 1962–1965. Director-General of the Industrial Co-operation Organization, 1966. Ambassador to Indonesia, 1966–1970. President of the mining and chemicals company directorate, 1970.
Responsibility Commission Member. In charge of Development Aid and Co-operation Policy; Community budgets; Financial Control.

Name
Ralf Dahrendorf
Nationality German **Born** 1929 Hamburg. Married to an English wife. Three children.
Background Educated in Berlin, Switzerland and Hamburg. Imprisoned by Gestapo 1944–1945. Studied philosophy and classical philology at Hamburg and the LSE where he was awarded a PhD. Until 1968 he was a member of the Social Democrat Party, but he then joined the Free Democrats and served in the Landtag of Baden-Wurttemberg until 1970. 1969–1970 Parliamentary Secretary of State for Foreign Affairs. Became a Commissioner in 1970 and was in charge of External Relations.
Responsibility Commission Member. In charge of Research; Science and Education (includes external relations in the scientific, technical and nuclear sectors); Dissemination of Technical and Scientific Information; Mutual Recognition of Diplomas; Joint Research Centre; Statistical Office. (Leaving in Autumn 1974 to be Director of the LSE.)

Name
Finn Olav Gundelach
Nationality Danish **Born** 1925. Married with two children.
Background Aarhus University. 1951 joined Ministry of Foreign Affairs. Served as Permanent Danish Representative at the United Nations European Headquarters in Geneva, and at the GATT Secretariat, Geneva, as head of the trade policy department and as Deputy Director General. In July 1967 he became head of the Danish Mission to the European Communities.
Responsibility Commission Member. In charge of Internal Market (includes removal of technical barriers to trade; right of establishment and freedom to supply services; harmonization of economic legislation; European Company Law); Administration of the Customs Union.

Name
Petrus Josephus Lardinois
Nationality Dutch **Born** 1924 Noorbeek. Married with five children.
Background Agricultural University in Wageningen. 1951 entered Government Agricultural Advisory Service. 1960–1963 Agricultural Attaché in London. 1963 elected member of Upper Chamber of Dutch States-General as representative of Roman Catholic Peoples' Party. October 1963 member of Council of Europe and of its agriculture and transport committees. 1967 Minister of Agriculture and Fisheries.
Responsibility Commission Member. In charge of Agriculture.

(See also pp. 92 and 160)

Section 4
**Introductions, comments and questions on
'Policy-making in Practice'–the 1965 crisis** Stephen Holt
and 'The Political Process' David Coombes

Contents

Course team introduction to 'Policy-making in Practice – the 1965 Crisis' (Stephen Holt)

In this extract from his book *The Common Market: The Conflict of Theory and Practice*, Stephen Holt outlines an incident in the history of the Communities which highlights the key question – where does power lie?

Some believe that the 1965 Crisis, as it is known, was deliberately provoked by Walter Hallstein, the Commission President, in order to 'clear the air' over the issue of supranationality. Others, that a crisis of the magnitude which emerged was inevitable in the run of events at that time (Dale, paragraph 18). Whichever viewpoint is taken, it is clear that a number of issues of principle were involved. As Holt says, the French thought it better 'to get the argument settled on a general level rather than getting involved in a specific and perhaps complicated issue' (p. 66).

As you read this short article, gaining a knowledge of the story is less important than understanding the principles which were at stake.

This article is to be found in the Reader on pages 66–74. Turn to it before reading further.

Comments and questions

Having studied this article you should be able to answer these questions (refer to the text if necessary). Comments on the questions will be found in the Supplementary Material under 'Further comments on Unit 2'.

6 Reformulate briefly the 'package deal' which was presented by the Commission to the Council. What controversial issue, central to the development of the Communities, did it attempt to deal with?

7 What form of words was devised to meet the French objections to the transition to majority voting? What limitation does this put on the decision-making 'power' of the Council?

8 From Holt's discussion of part of the French 'decalogue' of complaints against the Commission, note the ways in which the Commission had been attempting to extend its influence and power.

Course team introduction to 'The Political Process' (David Coombes)

An introduction to this article is to be found in the Reader (p. 58). Please read this as it sets the article into its original context.

As you read the article itself, note the ways in which the Commission has attempted to engage national ministers and civil servants in the decision-making process of the Community.

Before studying the comments and questions, turn to pages 58–66 of the Reader and read the article.

Comments and questions

Comments on these questions are to be found in the Supplementary Material under 'Further comments on Unit 2'.

9 Having read this article, list the ways in which the Commission engages members of national governments in the decision-making process and explain the reasoning behind it.

10 *Engrenage* is an important concept introduced in this article. Attempt a brief definition of it.

Section 5
Decision-making in the EEC
Michael Niblock

Contents

Michael Niblock graduated from the London School of Economics in 1962. After three years as a post-graduate student at London University, he lectured in politics at the University of Bristol between 1965 and 1968. He gained a PhD degree for a thesis on the consultative role of the European Parliament in Community decision-making in 1969. Since 1968 he has worked in the Conservative Research Department. He is author of *The EEC: National Parliaments in Community Decision-Making* published in 1971 in the joint European series of Political and Economic Planning and Chatham House. He wishes to emphasize that the views expressed in his paper are his own, and not necessarily those of any other person or organization.

Course team introduction

Michael Niblock picks up many of the issues raised so far in this unit. His general purpose is to examine the 'process' of decision-making in the Communities.

He continues the discussion of *engrenage* begun by David Coombes, and looks at the role of 'package deals', devised by the Commission, in producing agreement between the members and hence the progress of the Communities.

The article continues with a discussion of the powers of the Commission and the apparent contradiction between its roles as initiator and mediator noted by Coombes (Reader, p. 65).

Niblock then introduces another aspect of the decision-making process – the efforts of non-government groups to influence policy. This is discussed further by Hartley and Sidjanski (essential reading, Section 6) and in some of the other extracts in the Reader (recommended reading).

Niblock goes on to discuss some of the theoretical perspectives on decision-making which have been developed by political scientists. It is possible that you will find some of the concepts confusing so we suggest that you read through this section quickly, as Unit 4 returns to the issues raised.

The article concludes by posing the questions which will need to be answered as the enlarged Community develops over the next few years.

This introduction has outlined the article in some detail so that you will see, before reading it, how it overlaps with what has gone before. It will reinforce what you have already learned, by helping you to a clearer understanding of the relationships between the Community institutions, and between the institutions and other groups which participate in the decision-making process.

Decision-making in the EEC

Michael Niblock

1
Introduction
When the founder members of the original six-nation Community set up the organization in 1958 they had, when it came to deciding upon institutional arrangements, a choice between two courses: either institutions could be established which derived their authority from the governments of the member states, or a way could be devised of giving the Community a source of authority independent of that of the governments. The signatories chose the first alternative, though various provisions were written into the Treaty of Rome which suggested an evolution in the direction of the latter. As a result what was established in 1958 was an essentially inter-governmental system of decision-making – a feature which has been enhanced with the passage of time.

However, before embarking on its description an important dichotomy needs to be noted. If to the political scientists the key to the process is how consensus is reached between governments (Section 2.1), from the purely legal point of view the Community possesses characteristics which distinguish it sharply from other international organizations. To the lawyer the essential innovation of the Community Treaty is the power given to the institutions to pass rules applying directly in the member states without the intermediary of national institutions (Dale, Unit 2; Frankel,

Unit 3). Far from having been watered down during the period of the Community's existence this element of supranationality has been enhanced, lately by the European Court of Justice asserting that in the event of any conflict between Community Law and national law, Community Law takes priority (Mitchell, Unit 3).

In this paper we look at the community institutions from four main angles – 3
1 of their central purpose of reconciling opinion between member governments;
2 the role played in the process by the European Commission;
3 the point of view of those institutions and groups which are outside the central decision-making agency of the Commission and Council and seek to influence its activity; and
4 from the angle of the overall process of integration to which the institutions are intended to contribute. The final section asks a question about the future development of the institutions.

2 Consensus-building in the Community

Decisions in the Community are taken by the Commission and Council in partner- 4
ship. The Commission formulates proposals which then go before the Council for consideration. These two bodies are at the centre of a vast network of communications which link the Community to the national governments and administration, non-governmental interests as well as parliamentary bodies. Since decision-making depends essentially on the negotiation of agreements between governments, it is hardly surprising that in certain respects the Community process bears some resemblence to negotiating encounters in other international forums. Positions are taken up, warnings issued and alliances formed. 'Crises' are not infrequent. When they are resolved and agreement reached, everybody is proclaimed to be on the winning side.

The special features of the Community process derive in part from the role of the 5
Commission, which we look at in greater detail in Section 2 below, and in part from the extent, subject-matter and continuity of Community decision-making. The fact that the Community covers policy matters which have hitherto been regarded as 'domestic' has laid the basis for the involvement of national administrators in the process in what has been referred to as *engrenage* (Section 2.2). The fact that the Community is not an isolated negotiation on a limited range of issues but a continuous process of discussion and search for agreement across a wide field makes not only for a degree of understanding and respect for each other's goals and interests among the national governments; it provides as well the raw material for package deals. Before turning to these details it is worth summarizing in brief the process of decision as it occurs on matters of internal policy in the Community.

2.1 The process of decision

National administrations and other outside interests are brought into the process of 6
elaborating proposals at an early stage. The initial work is undertaken in the relevant Directorate General of the Commission. Before this has proceeded far and before the Commission's ideas have solidified in the form of a draft, the Commission convenes a meeting of experts from the national administrations to discuss the problems arising in the sector and the options open to the Community. Those who attend such meetings do so without binding their governments, though it is assumed that what they have to say bears some relation to the position subsequently to be taken up by their respective governments in the Council.

From the Commission's point of view, the purpose of such contacts, apart from any 7
technical advice or information which can be imparted to it, is the understanding that can thereby be gained of national standpoints which inevitably have to be taken into account in the drawing up of a proposal. The same purpose is served at a higher level by contacts which take place between the competent Commissioner and national ministers before an important proposal is submitted to the Council. At this stage the

Commission will also receive advice and opinions from interest groups and may well have discussed the matter in committees of the European Parliament (Dale, paragraph 8).

On being passed by the Commission and forwarded to the Council a proposal begins 8 a usually lengthy journey up the hierarchy of committees at the apex of which is the Council itself. It is at this stage that the government negotiating positions are taken up. The determination of a government attitude is itself likely to have involved a great deal of bargaining and discussion, this time within the national administrations between departments whose interests may differ over what the response of the government should be (Wallace, Unit 3). Governmental viewpoints will be put forward at three levels – that of the working group of experts, which does the detailed scrutiny of a proposal, the Committee of Permanent Representatives and at a later date at the ministerial level (Dale, Unit 2, Section 4.1).

On the Council's side consideration of a proposal proceeds by means of a sort of 9 vertical shuttle. Working groups report to the Committee of Permanent Representatives, which in turn reports to the Council. Very often the permanent representatives will refer a matter back to the working group for further discussion before submitting their own report to the Council and except on those rare occasions when the Council is able to reach its decision at one meeting there will be further reference back to the Committee of Permanent Representatives. The main function of the latter is to get as much agreement as possible on the text and where there is no alternative to leaving it to ministers, to settling points of dissension, to clarify the areas of disagreement and the options open. The vertical shuttle is complicated by the fact that there is also a lateral movement between the Commission and the Council and its subordinate bodies. The Commission is a full participant at all levels on the Council side. It will very often be asked for technical advice and for suggestions as to how conflicts can be resolved, with the right to amend its proposal at any time before the final decision is taken. Its initiative in this respect has often played a vital part in getting agreement in the Council (Dale, Unit 2, paragraphs 29–30).

2.2 *Engrenage* is rather inadequately translated into English as 'enmeshing' or 'gearing 10
Engrenage in'. It has been used to describe the way in which the institutions of the Community have sought to engage in the process of decision political actors not formally a part of the institutions.

The immediate effect of *engrenage* has been to produce a vast proliferation of com- 11 mittees and working groups of one kind or another. Some of these are convened under the auspices of the Commission, others meet under the umbrella of the Council; some exist to bring about close co-ordination between the governments and the member states on the application of Community rules, while others, such as the Consultative Committees set up covering different sectors of agricultural production are intended to assist co-operation between the Community and professional organizations.

Some have a purely consultative role. Others like the Agricultural Management 12 Committees have some much more precise powers.

The overall effect has been to engage a widening circle of national administrators 13 and other national actors in the processes of the Community.

One of the first academic observers to focus on the phenomenon of *engrenage* was 14 Leon Lindberg who judged it in a favourable light:

there is strong evidence that this sort of interaction contributes to a 'community minded-ness', by broadening perspectives, developing personal friendships, and fostering a

143

camaraderie of expertise, all of which come from being involved in a joint problem-solving operation. Such problems can be expected to occur in a rough correlation to the frequency of contact. Thus they are more marked in the Committee of Permanent Representatives which meets twice a week or more and is in constant contact with European integration affairs, than in one of the committees of customs experts that meets once or twice a year. (Lindberg, 1963, p. 286.)

The researches which Lindberg subsequently made into the attitudes of national 15 administrators, ministers and interest group leaders concerned with the form of the Common Agricultural Policy confirmed him in the view that at least in this area *engrenage* was leading to modes of thought and action favourable to integration. 'Actor socialization' was occurring (Lindberg, 1965).

Others have been more sceptical. David Coombes in particular has raised the 16 question as to whether there may not be a debit side to the account in the reduced ability of the Commission to play a forceful role in the Community (Coombes, 1970).

Contact with the Commission may help to inculcate 'European' attitudes among 17 national civil servants but is it not at least as likely that the Commission will be 'infected' by national sentiments? (Dale, paragraphs 7–10).

2.3 **Unanimity and the package deal**

That the Council of Ministers has chosen to take the greater part of its decisions by 18 unanimity, laying aside the legal possibility of majority votes, is due primarily to the unnaturalness of majority voting on a body such as the Council where the decision-makers are representatives of government and when all the effort early on in the process is directed towards reaching an overall consensus. Even if ministers could steel themselves to majority decisions, it is difficult to imagine the Committee of Permanent Representatives easily accustoming itself to this, so deeply ingrained in that body is the habit of consensus-building. For the Community which has no means of physical coercion at its disposal unanimity is a better guarantee of compliance than majority voting. For individual member governments it is basically a matter of enlightened self-interest. Today on issue x a government may have the Council majority on its side but there is no guarantee that tomorrow on issue y it will not be in a minority and needing the protection of the *de facto* unanimity rule.

The prevalence of unanimity has invariably been seen as evidence of the failure of 19 the governments to adopt 'European' attitudes and of the dominance of national interest in decision-making. So in a sense it is. But given the system that has been established it can also be taken as a sign of mutual sensitivity and responsiveness on the part of the governments.

Moreover, acceptance of unanimity would seem to be a necessary condition for that 20 vehicle of Community action – the package deal.

The main steps forward made by the Community in the 1960s were achieved as a 21 result of bargains between governments which linked a variety of decisions, not all of them in the same policy sector. The first marathon ending on 14 January 1962, for example, produced a package which included the first Community regulation on the rules of competition as well as certain important regulations in the agricultural sector. The marathon sessions of May and June 1966 resulted in decisions in agriculture, on industrial customs tariffs and social policy. The same technique has been used, less spectacularly and frequently with less success, in other areas such as transport policy (Lindberg and Scheingold, Reader, pp. 78–92).

The package deal has the obvious attraction that it widens the scope for com- 22 promise between the Council members. It makes it possible to reach agreement at a higher level than is implied in simply splitting the difference between the opposing points of view on a specific proposal. On the other hand, this method of taking decisions tends to a certain rigidity. It may not be easy to change one element in a package when circumstances might require, because of the disturbance that might be made to the balance of interest overall. Furthermore, reaching agreements in this way adds greatly to the remoteness of the Community institutions from ordinary people and the difficulties of comprehending what is going on between the governments. If we believe simplicity in decision-making is a virtue and an aid to democracy, the Community clearly does not share it.

A further decision-making tactic in the Community is the deadline – an agreement 23
to agree at a later date, with the date specified. Marathon sessions have invariably been conducted against time limits imposed in some cases by Treaty obligations and in others by subsequent agreements worked out between the governments. Not infrequently, deadlines have resulted from marathon sessions themselves, one movement forward thus providing the basis for a further one at a later date.

How far are these modes of political action, developed by the Community of the 24
Six during its fourteen years of existence, being carried over into the new enlarged community? There is every sign that they are being. The process of *engrenage* is as apparent in the Nine as in the Six and the reluctance to take decisions by majority vote no less great. Even before the new Community had formally come into being the member governments at the Paris Summit of October 1972 had agreed on a programme of action and a series of deadlines, which looked like providing the basis for some extensive package deals in the months ahead (Unit 1, Section 5.3).

3 Is the Commission a body with a political role or is it really no more than a secre- 25
The Commission – tariat? The first is the view which has been consistently held by European federalists,
political organ or who have seen in the Commission the embryo of a future federal executive. The
secretariat? second was the opinion of General de Gaulle to whom the Commissioners were 'mere technicians'. In the Gaullist view the Commission can play a vital part in furthering agreement between governments, but it has no right to manipulate the latter in the interests of political options of its own choosing. The clash between these two opposing views came out in the open in the second half of 1965 when the French Government boycotted the Community (Holt, Reader, pp. 66–74). The *casus belli* for this crisis was the submission by the Commission of an ambitious proposal the prime purpose of which was to get the French to pay for the agricultural finance rules they desired by concessions on the institutional side. To General de Gaulle this was a clear instance of the Commission exceeding the bounds of political propriety. From the resulting crisis in the Community, the Commission emerged with its legal powers basically intact but there was no going back to the political style which it had adopted in the early 1960s. The crisis revealed some of its institutional weaknesses.

The Commission has two main assets – its right of initiative and its ability, based 26
on its participation in the work of the Council at both ministerial and official levels, to act as mediator between the governments (Dale, paragraph 17). In addition, it has the possibility of gaining support for its view among other actors in the process, notably members of the European Parliament and organizations representing interests. However, it calls for political skills to exploit these assets, which are of themselves hardly sufficient to guarantee a role of major political influence for the Commission, and the particular skills required are essentially those of diplomacy rather than mass political action–defining objectives which are realistic in terms of what other parties will accept, understanding national interests, seeing how coalitions of support can be built up, and judging when the moment is propitious for action.

The potential of the Commission when such skills are employed was seen at its clearest in 1963–4 with respect to the so-called Mansholt Plan for harmonizing cereals prices in one stage. There was no obligation on the part of the Community to agree on a single level of cereals prices for implementation at a later date as it did in December 1964. Indeed it was assumed that this would be a step-by-step process taking place over a number of years. But by putting forward a proposal in December 1963 to harmonize in one step, the Commission effectively transformed the context in which the matter was being viewed by the Community governments and with the indispensible support of the French government, succeeded in achieving for the Community the significant objective of an agreement on the single level of prices by the end of the following year (Ritson, Unit 5). 27

The cereals price decision also illustrates the strength which the Commission can acquire by virtue of its acceptance as a mediator in the Council. Having made its proposal and after waiting for those governments who could be expected to support it to declare their stand, the Commission came forward in May 1964 with a modified proposal in the hope of allaying the fears of the German government from where the main opposition came. The same tactic was employed in early December, this time with Italian interests partly in mind. In neither case did the Commission have to alter in any fundamental way its original proposal. 28

The achievement of the Commission in 1963–4 lay in the success it had in combining the forceful pursuit of political objectives with mediation between the governments. *Prima facie* the two would not seem to be readily compatible, the danger being that the further a mediator goes in espousing particular political objectives the less acceptable is he liable to become in the capacity of conciliator. In fact the problem of the ambiguity of the Commission's role goes deeper than this, as David Coombes has elucidated in his book *Politics and Bureaucracy in the European Community* (Coombes 1970, chapter 10). Coombes, after noting the wide variety of roles that the Commission is supposed to fulfil, questions how far they can be satisfactorily combined in an organization constituted in the manner of the Commission and its administration. For example, the increasing administrative tasks which fall upon the Commission call for a structural hierarchical organization, but is this appropriate if it is to be effective as a source of political leadership? The mediatory function of the Commission may be helped by the close association with national administrations which results from *engrenage* but may such an organization not be too diffuse to formulate political goals? Coombes reaches the conclusion that the Commission as it is constituted is ill-suited to the task of evolving political guidelines and will become more so as its administrative tasks accumulate with the advance of integration. 29

The strengths and weaknesses of the Commission have also to be seen in relation to the nature of decision-making in the Community to date. When it has achieved a political impact it has been with respect to those decisions and choices which might be described as 'integrative' in other words, when the choice before the government has been whether or not a particular area of policy should be made a Community responsibility. As the institutionalized promoter of further integration – the 'guardian of the Treaty' – the Commission has shown persistency and at times imagination. However, it has been on much more uncertain ground when the question has changed from being one of 'should we integrate in policy area *x*' to one of 'having integrated *x*, what should the joint political objectives in that field be?'. The Commission is much less well adapted to a political role at this level, its main weakness being the lack of any direct channel of communication with public opinion through directly elected representatives. The contacts the Commission maintains with the European level interest groups, the formation of which it has done so much to encourage, and with the European Parliament are certainly valuable in bringing it in touch with a circle of opinion which is wider than that of the national governments, 30 but they are not a substitute for direct contact with those to whom Community decisions apply. The further integration advances the more is this deficiency likely to tell against the Commission.

4
Influencing the
decision-makers

There are two main groups of people who are interested in influencing the course of 31 decision-making – members of parliament and representatives of non-governmental interest groups. They seek to do so at two levels – at the national level and at that of the Community – and in two ways – using channels which are provided for in the Treaty on the one hand and through informal channels of communication on the other.

4.1
The national
Parliaments

Of all the potential influences the parliaments of the member states have been the 32 least active, even though they stand to lose most from the transference of authority from national institutions to the Community. The overwhelming support which has been given to European integration in the national parliaments for most of the time has tended to militate against a high level of parliamentary activity or the energetic pursuit of governments on Community issues. It is already clear that the Westminster Parliament is not going to follow quite the same pattern of passive behaviour. The heated Parliamentary controversies which occurred at Westminster in 1970–2 on the question of joining the EEC are, now that Britain is in the organization, being carried over to some extent to specific issues as they arise. At the time of writing it remains to be seen how the Westminster Parliament will decide to exercise a scrutiny over Community affairs and the government's handling of European policies. Various procedures for keeping Parliament informed have been accepted by the government on the recommendation of a select committee set up to consider the problem, but in the opinion of many these need to be supplemented by arrangements which enable community legislation to be looked at in detail by one or more select committees.

Of the parliaments of the original six member states the most consistent watch on 33 community issues has been kept in the Dutch Lower House and the German Parliament. In West Germany a formal procedure exists whereby the main Community drafts are transmitted to Parliament. In the *Bundestag* (the Lower House) they are looked at in the competent committee whose opinion is contained in a report to the plenary assembly. Only rarely are these reports debated in the *Bundestag* as a whole. In the Netherlands it is normal for important Commission proposals to be discussed in the competent committee of the Lower House in the presence of the minister before he goes to the EEC Council to present his country's point of view. The minister may also be invited back after the Council has reached its decision to give an explanation of how it did so. A similar procedure is not unknown in the Belgian Parliament, though it appears to be applied a good deal less systematically (Niblock, 1971).

It has for long been the experience of parliamentary bodies that their control over the 34 executive is weakest when the latter is engaged in negotiating an agreement with a third party. In such a situation there is a limit to what parliament can be told about the government's intentions and what it is prepared to settle for around the negotiating table. As Mr John Davies, Chancellor of the Duchy of Lancaster and Minister responsible for co-ordinating Britain's European policy said in one of the early parliamentary debates held on a sensitive Community issue in the spring of 1973:

In defending the interests of the country to the best of his ability in the Councils of the Community, the minister needs to be in a flexible position to negotiate. Flexibility for negotiating is essential. (House of Commons, Hansard, 3 April 1973, col. 291).

Since the Community involves a continuous process of bargaining between the governments, the presumption against the adoption of rigid positions by any one government is all the greater. Moreover, unlike other international agreements, Community agreements or at least the great majority of them do not have to go through any process of ratification at the national levels. Hence even if a national parliament does dissent from a Community settlement there is from the strictly legal point of view little that it can do about it. On the other hand it remains the case in all national systems that governments cannot neglect parliamentary opinion. The ultimate sanction of dismissal is there; short of that, parliamentary restiveness is something most governments wish to avoid when possible. National parliaments are obviously not capable of exercising any finely tuned influence on community decision-making but they are part of the 'opinion base' on which governments have to found their policies (Mackintosh, Reader, pp. 129–38).

35

4.2 The European Parliament

Those members of the national parliaments who sit in the European Parliament belong to a consultative body whose main links are with the European Commission and which has succeeded in establishing only the most tenuous relationship with the Council of Ministers. Little attempt has been made to date to harmonize the interaction of the European Parliament with the Commission with that of individual national Parliaments vis-à-vis their respective Council members.

36

In a number of ways the European Parliament has improved its position in the institutions since 1958. Its right to give an opinion on Community drafts has been extended. It has established a close working relationship with the Commission whose members are regular attenders at sessions of the European Parliament either to speak in debates or answer questions in a manner reminiscent of ministers before national parliaments. Within parliamentary committees the practice has grown up of frequent exchanges of opinion with members of the Commission, who frequently take the committee into their confidence when talking about future plans and intentions. Moreover, the Commission has gone along with the Parliament's wishes that it include any amendments which Parliament has made to proposals and which are acceptable to the Commission in revised proposals to the Council. But the fact remains that the European Parliament cannot bind the Commission to its opinion. It cannot force it to accept an amended version of the proposal any more than one of the governments can be bound to a particular position by its national parliament. Indeed as a potential mediator in the Council the Commission's need for flexibility is even greater than is that of government.

37

The Parliament has the power to censure the Commission but since European-minded parliamentarians see in the Commission the best hope of advancing the process of integration this is a somewhat theoretical right. It has not been used to date. Though the European Parliament has at times been a fertile source of suggestions and ideas and has left its mark on a number of important Community decisions, its ability to set parameters or confines to the exercise by the Council of its decision-making powers has been virtually non-existent.

38

4.3 Interest groups

It follows from the way decisions are taken in the Community that non-governmental interests in the member states are provided with a variety of points of access to the system for the exercise of pressure. These exist at the national level and at that of the Community. Within the formal framework of the Treaty a forum for the representation of interests is provided in the Economic and Social Committee on which a broad range of social and economic interests are represented (Dale, Section 8.4). Moreover, since 1958, several hundred organizations representing particular interests to the Commission have been formed and have set up offices in Brussels. Some of these such as the trade union organizations, the farmers' unions, and the

39

employers' organizations have well-developed channels with the Commission and engage in regular and intensive contacts with Commissioners and their officials (Reader, Section 3).

A national group representing a particular sector of industry, for example the chemical industry or engineering, is likely to have no less than five avenues through which it can seek to exert influence on Community decision-makers: 40

1 Direct contact with the national government and competent departments in particular.

2 Contacts with the competent departments of national government through the wider grouping of the national employers' organization.

3 Representation to the Commission through the European level organization, which exists to represent the interests of the industrial sector.

4 Representation to the Commission through the European level employers' organization.

5 Representation to the Community institutions through the Economic and Social Committee, assuming that the group has a representative on that body, or somebody who can put forward its views (Reader, pp. 143–9).

An active pressure group is not likely to neglect any of these channels, but in which direction it will make the main effort will naturally depend on the variety of factors. If an interest group knows from bitter experience that the likelihood of its being heard sympathetically by a national government department is small, it is obviously going to be more inclined to explore the possibilities of influence at the Community level than a group which has a well established relationship of confidence with a national government department. The latter group will be forced back on its national means of pressure if its affiliates in Community level organizations tend to take a divergent view on issues of importance to x. 41

The wider the European grouping, clearly the greater the probability that an individual national interest group will see its objectives watered down in the search for consensus between the members. If this, combined with the fact that Community decision-making is the prerogative of national government representatives, is an argument for concentrating pressure groups actively at the national level, sectional interests can hardly afford to neglect the fact that the process of decision in the Community begins in the Commission, with the drawing up of a proposal. If only to keep in touch with initiatives of the Commission, some means of communication and contact in Brussels is highly desirable. 42

Whether it is faced by interest groups or by parliamentarians, the problem of exerting pressure in the Community shares one common characteristic, the lack of any one quarter where the exertion of influence, if effective, can be decisive. The fact is that there is no such single focus of power. Influence on the Commission, that is the concern of the Community level groups, is far from being a guarantee that action along any particular lines will follow. If a national government is persuaded to a point of view, there are eight other governments and the Commission who are there to push developments in a contrary direction. Superficially, the diversity of points of contact is advantageous for pressure groups, but it is symptomatic of a profound characteristic of the Community system, namely the diffusion of responsibility, and this is much less commendable. 43

5
The 'dynamics' of
European integration
There has been no uniformity in the development of the Community. In some areas, notably agriculture, the objectives of the Treaty have by and large been achieved; in others progress has been at best sluggish, and at worst non-existent. In seeking to 44

explain these variations in performance, political scientists have looked to the concept of 'spillover', but as with other concepts in social science, this one has become the subject of different usages (Barber, Unit 4).

A common element in the different meanings attached to 'spillover' is the notion that for one reason or another a measure of integration in one area of policy acts as an incentive to integrate in other areas. Taking some guidance from the writing of Leon Lindberg and Stuart Scheingold on this subject, it is possible to distinguish four main types of 'spillover', depending on the nature of the impulse for further integrations (Lindberg and Scheingold, 1970, Chapter 4). 45

5.1 Functional spillover

This is based on the logical connections which can be seen to exist between different aspects of policy, especially in the general area of economic policy – or what Hallstein once referred to as the 'absolute inner unity of all economic policy'. It postulates that the achievement of a major integration in one area (for example the creation of an industrial customs union) will give rise to problems (for example, how to control economic life in the situation of greatly increased economic interdependence) that can only be satisfactorily dealt with by further measures of co-operation and integration (in this case the closer harmonization of economic policies between the member states). 46

Functional spillover does not of itself postulate that the further measures of integration will necessarily be taken, only that a presumption in favour of them is created. Whether or not they are taken will depend on the political will of the decision-makers. If this is deficient, then it is quite conceivable there will not be spillover but 'spillback' – i.e. the member states will make a retreat from the integration that they have achieved, in the face of the functional problems to which it has given rise. 47

5.2 Political spillover

This variant of the concept postulates that governments that are members of the developing community will provide momentum to the process of integration by seeking to compensate for losses they suffer in one field by trying to extend integration in other areas where they stand to gain. They will be better able to do this if they are able to invoke functional spillover as a reason why the Community should extend its field of activities. Their readiness to promote political spillover is likely to be related to what Lindberg and Scheingold refer to as 'actor socialization' and 'feedback'. 48

5.3 Actor socialization

This relates to the attitudes of immediate participants in the decision-making process, whether they be national ministers – or national officials. It is supposed that by taking part in the Community they will develop attitudes and perceptions which will make them favourable to further allocations of responsibility to the organization, following the initial allocation to which they have contributed. 49

5.4 Feedback

This will occur when groups outside the decision-making process who have nevertheless been affected by it, and who are liable to be, begin to make demands on the Community system for further action at the Community level. Such groups become accustomed to think of the Community as an organization through which their own sectional interests can be advanced. 50

During the 1960s functional spillover was variously over-estimated and underestimated, depending very much on the state of morale prevailing in the Community at the time. In the mid-1960s before the French boycott of the institutions, many began talking about it as though it were a quasi-automatic process, suggesting, for example, that the agreement on the common cereals price in December 1967 made 51 it virtually impossible for countries to change their exchange rates. This as it turned out was turning logic on its head! On the other hand, when stagnation beset the Community in the late 1960s there was a tendency to play it down whereas a number of developments particularly in the field of economic co-operation between the governments were a clear reflection of functional importance.

However, much the more powerful influence has been in 'political spillover', combined with the interaction which has occurred between the Community and non-member countries. Early on it was pressures on the Community from Britain and EFTA countries that were largely responsible for forcing the member states to agree on a basic policy towards the outside world. Later the Kennedy Round exerted a powerful integrating influence, partly because it required the Community to adopt a common position on important issues, and partly because of the link-up made with aspects of the Community's internal development. More recently one has seen in the Community's response to the monetary and trade challenge of the United States the effect, albeit uncertain at first, in favour of a more closely integrated Community. 52

The indispensible fuel to the process and integration in the 1960s was provided by the French government's aim of extending the Common Market to agriculture – a policy which was pursued with a ruthless determination and with a full panoply of bargaining ploys, including the threat to withdraw from the Community organizations. The other governments were given the choice between a Community with an agricultural policy and no Community at all – in fact a Hobson's choice for them given their commitment to European integration. 53

The German government, which stood to lose most from the proposed Common Agricultural Policy was determined to gain advantages elsewhere. It looked primarily to the further development of the customs union and freer international trade. This laid the basis for a series of deals in the 1960s linking agriculture with other policy areas, beginning in 1960 with the agreement to accelerate the achievements of the industrial customs union, and at the same time to make more rapid progress towards the Common Agricultural Policy. In the mid-1960s the main link-up was with the Kennedy Round negotiations, the cereals price decision of December 1964 being made politically possible for the Germans by the fact that the previous month the French government had made concessions enabling the talks on industrial tariff cutting to get underway. In the late 1960s the tie-up was with the enlargement negotiations so long desired by the other five governments. In late 1969 the French government of President Pompidou made their agreement to open negotiations with Britain and the other candidate countries dependent on the so-called 'deepening' of the Community, by which they meant an agreement on the long-term rules for financing the agricultural policy. A further example of political spillover on this occasion arose from the fact that not for the first time in the history of the Community the Italian government took a strong eleventh-hour stand in favour of an Italian interest. As a result the December 1969 marathon resulted in agreement to establish a common market in wine. 54

We have already referred to the role which the Commission is capable of playing as 'logroller' in the Community bargaining process. In the related fields of agricultural policy, the Industrial Customs Union and international tariff cutting, the Commission used this means of influence to balance interests and build up a consensus which enabled progress to be achieved over a wide area. Its failure to do the same thing in the field of transport is put forward by Lindberg and Scheingold as one reason why the Community fell far short of meeting its objectives in this sector. In the estimation of these two authors the Commission failed to exploit functional spillovers where they existed, and made the serious initial mistake of putting forward proposals which did not have the support of the country which had the greatest 55

151

stake in the common transport policy, namely the Netherlands (Reader, pp. 78–92).

Without any governmental support comparable to that which was given by France 56 to the achievement of the Common Agricultural Policy, it was not surprising that political momentum behind the creation of a common transport policy has been lacking.

This brief analysis suggests some of the questions which are likely to be of import- 57 ance determining the future development of the enlarged Community in the years ahead.

First, is functional spillover going to make itself strongly felt, and if so in which 58 sectors? Secondly, what sort of political spillovers are foreseeable, and is any government going to provide the same sort of basic impetus behind future integration as did the French government in the 1960s? Thirdly are 'feedback' and 'actor socialization' going to be more significant forces than they appeared to have been in the Community of the Six? Fourthly, how skilful is the Commission going to prove itself in deploying 'logrolling' techniques; and lastly, are external relations going to prove an integrating influence on the Community as they were in the 1960s or might they conceivably become a force for disruption and disintegration?

On the answer to these questions will depend in large part what substance is given 59 to those principle aspirations to which the leaders of the nine-nation Community gave expression in the Paris Summit Communiqué of October 1972 (Unit 1, Section 5.3).

6 The institutional dilemma of the Community

The Community is a system of government based on consent, and as such it remains 60 effective only so long as the political decisions that it makes are respected by those to whom they are intended to apply (which is partly member governments and partly individuals and groups within the member states). In the Community system as it exists today, respect for decisions derives from the fact that they are taken by the governments. It is hardly too much to say that the peoples of the Community states support the Community because the governments do, and the latter have insured against the loss of support by the oft-criticized practice of taking decisions by unanimity.

If, by drawing directly on the authority of the governments, the Community 61 institutions enjoy a certain underlying strength two question marks nevertheless hang over them. The first concerns the capacity of the institutions to take decisions in conditions of advanced economic integration. To date the Community has had moderate success as a decision-maker. But, apart from the creation of a Common Agricultural Policy, which as we have suggested above is incomprehensible without reference to the basic political forces at work between the governments in the 1960s, its main achievements have been in the field of what has been called 'negative integration', i.e. the removal of barriers and acts of discrimination, rather than as a policy-maker in the true sense.

The Community is far from having proven itself as a system which is capable of 62 making meaningful political choices in areas where a substantial measure of integration has been achieved. If in the future it cannot meet expectations in this regard – if it appears that instead of giving authority to common institutions which can exercise it to the greater common benefit, integration means the creation of a decision-making vacuum – support for the system is liable to dissipate. This is all the more likely given the second question-mark over the institutional system – its remoteness from ordinary people. The EEC, as we noted at the outset, combines intergovernmentalism in decision-making with 'supranationalism' as a source of decisions which apply directly in the member states. Yet the institutional system is

152

hardly designed to elicit any active support or loyalty from the mass of the people who are liable to be affected by its decisions, and there is little to suggest that it has, against the odds, done this in practice.

Is then the answer, as the federalists advocate, to create immediately a link between governors and governed in the Community by electing the European Parliament by direct suffrage, with a federal cabinet responsible to it? One would be more confident that this was the answer if there was stronger evidence that there had grown up in western Europe a political 'community' which was in a true sense European. Instead what we have is still a number of national political communities. Politics is still carried on in essentially national compartments with national institutions as the main foci of loyalty. Contrary to what is sometimes maintained, present Community institutions have done little to break down this compartmentalization. 63

The existence of European-level organizations for interest groups does not alter the fact that people still look to their national institutions as the main defender of their well-being; and is it not after all the national governments that are expected to stand up in Community deliberations for the national interest? The question is thus whether federalism can be expected to create a sense of political community or common well-being, where that is absent, or at best only faintly perceptible. Our own view is that federal institutions may help to consolidate a sense of community between people, once this has by and large been achieved, but being themselves only a reflection of the political realities of the environment in which they operate, they can really do no more than this. 64

How the Community overcomes this institutional dilemma in the years ahead is in part a question of timing. There can be little doubt that if European integration is to develop to fulfil the aspirations that have been subscribed to by the governments in, notably, the Paris Summit Communiqué of October 1972, the institutions will have to begin to draw authority directly from the people. But until this can be done without the risk of jeopardizing what has been achieved and preventing further achievement, the means of improving the institutions must probably be sought in the direction of strengthening the European Parliament as an indirectly elected body, and devising additional channels of communication between the Community and the people of the member states. 65

References

Coombes, David (1970) *Politics and Bureaucracy in the European Community*, London, Allen and Unwin.

Lindberg, Leon (1963) *The Political Dynamics of European Economic Integration*, Stanford, Stanford University Press.

Lindberg, Leon (1965) *Decision-making and Integration in the European Community*, International Organisation, Winter 1965.

Lindberg, Leon and Scheingold, Stuart (1970) *Europe's Would-Be-Polity*, Englewood-Cliffs, Prentice-Hall.

Niblock, Michael (1971) *EEC – National Parliaments in Community Decision-making*, London, Chatham House/PEP.

Comments and questions

Having read and studied this paper you should attempt these questions. Comments on them will be found in the Supplementary Material under 'Further comments on Unit 2'.

11 Write down *four* main functions of the Commission with a very brief explanation of each.

12 In relation to the way the Commission operates which of the following attributes would you classify as 'strong' and which as 'weak'. Give reasons for your answer.
  a Responsiveness to the public.
  b Ability to initiate policies.
  c Ability to mediate between member states.
  d Guardians of the Treaty.
  e Quick decision-making.
  f Ability to persuade individual governments to abandon strongly held stands on particular issues.

13 Niblock writes of the 'institutional dilemma of the Community'. Summarize briefly what he means by that in four or five points.

Further reading

David Coombes (1970) *Politics and Bureaucracy in the European Community*, London, Allen and Unwin.

Stephen Holt (1967) *The Common Market – Conflict of Theory and Practice*, London, Hamish Hamilton.

Leon Lindberg (1963) *The Political Dynamics of European Economic Integration*, Stanford, Stanford University Press.

Leon Lindberg and Stuart Scheingold (1970) *Europe's Would-Be-Polity*, Englewood-Cliffs, Prentice-Hall.

Michael Niblock (1971) *EEC – National Parliaments in Community Decision-making*, London, Chatham House/PEP.

Emil Noël (1967) 'The Committee of Permanent Representatives', *Journal of Common Market Studies*, Vol. 5.

Emil Noël and Henri Étienne (1971) 'The Permanent Representatives Committee and the "Deepening" of the Communities,' *Government and Opposition*, Vol. 6, No. 4.

Dusan Sidjanski and Jean Meynaud (1971) *Les Groupes de Préssion dans la Communauté Européenne 1958–1968*, Brussels, Editions de L'Institut de Sociologie.

Section 6
**Introduction and Comments on
'Pressure groups and the European
Economic Community'** Dusan Sidjanski
and 'Transnational Political Forces' A. Hartley

Course team introduction and comments

Dusan Sidjanski 'Pressure Groups and the European Economic Community'
A. Hartley 'Transnational Political Forces'

These two articles should be read consecutively – Sidjanski first (Reader, pp. 166–73), followed by Hartley (Reader, pp. 139–43). They both deal with the phenomena of *European* interest groups and *European* parties.

Sidjanski outlines four phases in the formation of European interest groups related to four phases in the construction of European institutions – OEEC, ECSC, EEC and EFTA. He then proceeds to examine the relations between these groups and the Commission. He concludes with a discussion of the activities of the groups in the dynamic political system of the Communities which is transforming their powers and structures.

Hartley picks up and extends Sidjanski's discussion of the relationship between the European groups and the political parties. He advances the thesis that 'it is probable that embryonic European parties will spring rather from the pressure groups . . . than from the parochial political formations of individual countries' (p. 142).

As you read these two articles concentrate not on the details of particular pressure groups and parties, but on:

a identifying the ways Europe-wide groups organize to exert influence on the Community decision-making process, and

b listing the reasons for the apparent failure of the political parties to link-up effectively.

There is much more information on these two issues in the other articles in the Reader (these are recommended reading for this unit). Some of these issues are discussed in Television programme 1: 'Pressure groups at work'.

156

Section 7
Conclusion to Unit 2
and self-assessment activities

At the outset of this unit, on page 87, we set five objectives for you to aim at while working through the essential readings. Check these objectives to see whether you can achieve them to your satisfaction at this stage of the course. The purpose of the activities set out here is to remind you of some of the key points which are made in the readings, and to help you consolidate your learning.

Further comments on these questions and activities are to be found in the Supplementary Material under 'Further comments on Unit 2'.

14 Write down the names of five Commissioners and the areas of Community activity for which they are responsible.

15 In describing the Council of Ministers would you say:

a   Each member state appoints a permanent minister who attends each Council meeting.

b   Decision-making is still largely based on the need to reconcile conflicting interests.

c   The Presidency of the Council is usually given to the individual minister who holds a decisive voice in the Council's affairs.

d   A leak to the news media during marathon sessions is a common way for a Minister to explain his position or justify his views.

16 Draw a flow chart showing how the following groups and institutions are linked together (take for example a decision on agriculture):

a   Council of Ministers.

b   Committee of Permanent Representatives.

c   European Parliament.

d   Ministries of member states.

e   Pressure groups.

f   The Commission.

17 Write down very briefly an explanation of 'Coreper' and its activities.

18 Both the Court of Justice and the Commission have been described as 'watchdogs'. Note briefly the similarities and differences you see between the institutions in fulfilling this role

19 Explain very briefly the present method of elections for members of the European Parliament, and say how this differs from the system preferred as ideal by the Treaty of Rome.

20 'The British Parliament is basically a two-party system. In the Commons the two major rival groups sit facing each other, with the executive government of the day drawn from the party with a majority. If that majority goes, the government falls, and a new election is held.' Covering as far as possible the points made in this quotation write a similar description of the European Parliament.

21 Outline briefly why you think some pressure groups have been more successful in organizing themselves on a Community basis than political parties.

22 If you were one of the following people, note down (in descending order of priority) some of the people you would contact if you wished to influence a Community decision:

a   A housewife concerned about the rising cost of food.

b   A local government official concerned with regional aid.

c   A shop steward wanting to encourage worker participation.

d   A businessman hoping to influence decisions on non-tariff barriers.

Some Members of the Commission

Name
Henri Simonet
Nationality Belgian   **Born** 1931 Brussels. Married with two children.
Background Free University of Brussels graduate. Taught law and economics at the University. 1961–1965 served successively as *Chef de Cabinet* to the Minister of Economic Affairs and of Energy, and to the Vice-Premier. 1966–1972 Socialist Member of Belgian Parliament. January 1972 Minister of Economic Affairs.
Responsibility Commission Vice-President. In charge of Taxation; Financial Institutions (banking and insurance); Harmonization of Company Law; Energy Policy; Euratom Safeguards and Control; Euratom Supply Agency.

Name
Altiero Spinelli
Nationality Italian   **Born** 1907 Rome
Background Studied law at Rome University. 1927 sentenced to ten years in prison and six years in exile for anti-Fascist activities. 1943 took part in the resistance and founded European Federalist Movement. 1948–1962 Secretary-General of EFM in Italy. 1966 Director of Rome Institute of International Affairs. 1968–1969 European Adviser to Foreign Minister Pietro Nenni. Became Commissioner in 1970.
Responsibility Commission Member. In charge of Industrial and Technological Policy.

Name
George Thomson
Nationality British   **Born** 1921 Stirling. Married with two children.
Background Dux (leading scholar) at Grove Academy, Dundee. Joins RAF in 1939 and serves until 1945. After the war he became a journalist, continuing his writing after entering Parliament as MP for Dundee East in 1952. 1959–1963 Opposition Spokesman on Commonwealth and Colonial Affairs. During the Labour Governments of 1964–1970 he held office as Minister of State at the Foreign Office; Secretary of State for Commonwealth Affairs and Minister without Portfolio. In October 1969 he became Chancellor of the Duchy of Lancaster and Deputy to the Secretary of State for Foreign and Commonwealth Affairs, with special responsibility for European Affairs. He conducted the British approach to the Communities up to the application to join in 1967, and again as Chancellor of the Duchy of Lancaster in 1969–1970. After the General Election of 1970 he led the Opposition in the House of Commons on Defence until April 1972 when he resigned from the Shadow Cabinet over the Community membership issue.
Responsibility Commission Member. In charge of Regional Policy.

(See also pp. 92 and 134)